THE FUTURE
OF THE CHINA MARKET

AEI-Hoover
policy studies

The studies in this series are issued jointly
by the American Enterprise Institute
for Public Policy Research and the Hoover
Institution on War, Revolution and Peace.
They are designed to focus on
policy problems of current and future interest,
to set forth the factors underlying
these problems and to evaluate
courses of action available to policymakers.
The views expressed in these studies
are those of the authors and do not necessarily
reflect the views of the staff, officers
or members of the governing boards of
AEI or the Hoover Institution.

THE FUTURE OF THE CHINA MARKET

Prospects for Sino-American Trade

Edward Neilan
Charles R. Smith

American Enterprise Institute for Public Policy Research
Washington, D. C.

Hoover Institution on War, Revolution and Peace
Stanford University, Stanford, California

78- 1302
AEI-Hoover Policy Study 11, August 1974
Second printing, January 1975
(Hoover Institution Studies 46)

ISBN 0-8447-3137-4
Library of Congress Catalog Card No. 74-13361

Printed in United States of America

Contents

1
Introduction

For us, ourselves, the most important thing is to handle China's affairs well. For a country like China, with so large a population, it will take us several decades to develop our economy. That won't be done during the twentieth century. We will need millions of trained successors to carry on this program.

Chou En-lai
November 1973

American businessmen have commented on the lack of reliable information about the China market. The proliferation of "how-to-trade-with-China" publications since President Nixon's visit to Peking in 1972 was, they felt, marked by hasty preparation and scant substantive guidance for prospective traders. The few good studies on the subject were priced too high for the businessman who wanted to get the "feel" of the China market before plunging in. These American comments were echoed by Chinese officials whom the authors met during several visits to China in 1972 and 1973. These officials were surprised, to say the least, at some of the misinformation that was dispensed in 1971 and 1972 in books on China trade.

The approaches of American university and government economists to the question of the future of U.S.-China trade have been too conservative and constrained by methodology which assumed China's tomorrow would be much like China's yesterday.

Writing about China is extremely difficult, considering the differences in culture and the inability of foreigners to probe beneath the surface of Chinese policy thinking. It takes audacity to try to forecast

1

what Sino-American trade will be ten or twenty years from now, when Chinese feelings on this subject are virtually a state secret.[1]

Another vital consideration is that in 1972 there came radical changes in the foreign policies of both China and the U.S. when President Nixon visited China and the rapprochement between the two countries began. One of the most important matters discussed during the visit was an increase in trade, and since then there has been a sharp rise in Sino-U.S. trade. Largely because of this unforeseen circumstance, earlier trade predictions have turned out to be far too conservative.

At the end of 1973, for example, total trade between the United States and China was $753.1 million. That is more than most American forecasters had predicted for 1980! The total would have been more had most-favored-nation (MFN) status been granted to the Chinese in time for American importers to purchase more Chinese goods without paying what amounted to exorbitant surcharges.[2]

There must be more imaginative approaches to viewing trade prospects, approaches that go beyond juggling statistics. Many of the attempts to chart China's trade future have been hampered by over-emphasis on what China did twenty and thirty years ago. These figures are valuable as a starting point but past performances should not be given so much weight. China's developmental pattern is showing improvement, and we believe that the gains over the next quarter-century will stagger the most imaginative Western thinkers.

There are many problems and potential pitfalls that could cause China's economic program to falter. Among them are the military and subversive threats from the Soviet Union, internal power struggles—particularly after Mao Tse-tung dies—the seeming disinclination of some nations to allow China to play a leading role in world affairs, natural calamities, and others.

In the future, students of the Chinese economy and Peking's foreign trade will have to consider such subtleties as the long-term effects of changing values in Chinese society, including the attitudes and work styles of the Chinese masses as industry expands. Which models, ours

---

[1] *The China Letter*, no. 25 (November 1973), published in Hong Kong, reported that China plans to begin publishing in 1974 a new periodical devoted to foreign trade. A monthly, *China's Foreign Trade*, was discontinued in the late 1960s.

[2] A study by Steven C. Haas (*Impact of MFN on U.S. Imports from the PRC*, Office of East-West Trade, Department of State, 17 August 1973) estimated that granting of MFN would raise U.S. imports from the P.R.C. by 16 percent.

or theirs, should be used to compare the progress of Shensi No. 1 Textile Plant of China vs. Burlington Mills of the U.S.?

Could it be that gross national product (GNP) is not the valid "bottom line" measurement of a society's output that Western economists have suggested? On the other hand, are there some problems built-in to a socialist economy such as China's that will cause it to fail no matter what is done by the central management?

Will China someday be willing to depart from socialistic economic principles to aid development? Can actions, such as the granting of long-term credits by Western nations, contribute to political stability in such a way as to entice Peking away from the strictly socialist path?

Will the Soviet Union sit idly by and watch China become a strong economic power, showing up some of Moscow's failures?

What about Taiwan? Can Taiwan's success be transplanted to the mainland someday through a wedding of free enterprise and socialism by apolitical Chinese managers?

Now that the authors have visited China, they are convinced that there are no China "experts" in the West. But there can be serious students of China, and one area which should receive more serious attention is foreign trade.

It was with this in mind that the authors undertook this study. It is hoped that it will stimulate those who have an interest in China's foreign trade to pursue the subject more thoroughly.

All of the answers about the future of the China market are not in these pages. In fact, there are not very many answers here at all. The authors have tried to sort out the best thinking and writing on the subject, with the idea of presenting pegs on which to hang thoughts about the future.

Whether or not one believes the prediction that the twenty-first century will belong to the Chinese, it can at least be assumed that China will play a much bigger role in the international order by then than it does now. So we must consider the Sino-American future boldly and with imagination.

What are the possibilities that China's most plentiful natural resource—people—will someday be the labor-intensive work force that produces clothing for the entire world? Could this vast labor force be used to staff dozens of free-trade zones along China's coast, turning out light industrial products, as has been done in Taiwan?

3

What are the implications of a China fully opened to international tourism? What effect will expanded trade with China have on the American market? What will it mean when Shanghai No. 1 radios sell for less in St. Louis than do Sony radios? Or will Sonys someday be assembled in Shanghai at lower labor cost and then exported?

These questions are not based on idle speculation but are serious possibilities for the future. There are many, many more.

Someday before the end of this century, China's trading volume with the United States will be larger than that between Japan and the U.S. today. Needless to say, this prospect is fraught with important implications for political, social and economic interchange between Chinese and Americans.

2
Gauging Sino-American Trade Prospects

China's Economy: A Brief Perspective

"China has stood up."

Chairman Mao Tse-tung's words dramatize China's emergence as a strong nation mastering its own fate after a century of humiliation. Since 1949, the leadership of the People's Republic of China (P.R.C.) has managed to organize the largest single society in the world, feed more than 800 million people and direct them on a course of nation-building—no small accomplishment in itself.

China's Developmental Base. No one in the West pretends that China's development since 1949 has been free of mistakes or misjudgments or that the cost in human terms has not been high. But considering the challenge facing the leadership in 1949, progress has been considerable. There is still the possibility of decisive failure, perhaps through economic chaos or regional political splintering or both. But China has never before in modern times had a better base than now from which to move ahead in the world with strength and self-respect.

In addition to organizing and feeding one-quarter of mankind, the P.R.C. has vigorously pursued an economic policy of military-industrial expansion, agricultural collectivization, national self-sufficiency and what some have called consumer egalitarianism. The results of these policies have been mixed: some successes, some failures, some changes of direction, a lot of unfinished tasks.

If, in the long view, the general results of the Chinese experiment since 1949 can be said to have been impressive, they must also be said to have been erratic. Two periods of social and political upheaval—the

Great Leap Forward of the late 1950s and the Cultural Revolution of the late 1960s—interrupted the momentum of growth. The political pendulum in China has swung from apparent calm to turbulence and back with consequent disruptions in economic growth.

After a long period of isolation, the P.R.C. has cautiously re-emerged on the world scene, with many new diplomatic and economic relationships being established in the last few years.

Improved Sino-American Relations. Relations between the United States and the P.R.C. have steadily improved following President Nixon's February 1972 visit. In May 1973, liaison offices were set up in the respective capital cities. Trade ties between the two nations have expanded rapidly. U.S. businessmen are visiting the semiannual Canton (now called Kwangchow) Trade Fair in increasing numbers, and recently the National Council for United States-China Trade was formed in Washington to stimulate the continued expansion of trade.

It is difficult to grasp fully just how big China is or how large are the dimensions of its problems. China's population is estimated at some 800 to 850 million people, and is increasing at around 2 percent per year. Each year, therefore, China must absorb an additional population of some sixteen million, the equivalent of the populations of the Netherlands and Denmark combined.

One out of every four babies born into the world is Chinese. Per capita income in China is very low—about $150—but there are so many people that total GNP amounts to about $130 billion. This is larger than that of the United Kingdom.

China's size and enormous diversity have complicated the task of developing its economic potential, as have sharp shifts of economic policy. Nevertheless, there has been progress over the past quarter-century, as is indicated by an average annual real growth rate in total GNP of about 4 to 5 percent, and in per capita GNP of about 2 to 3 percent.

With the end of the Cultural Revolution in mid-1968, industrial production surged upward. Plant capacity was more fully utilized, and new facilities added earlier were finally brought into production. The pace slackened somewhat in 1972 as a reaction to the abnormally high growth rates of the preceding two years. Even so, the reported 8 percent rise of industrial output for 1972 is still high by most standards. Preliminary indications are that brisk growth continued in 1973.

The poor harvest of 1972 was a special disappointment to China's leaders. Grain output was down 4 percent, as both the rice and wheat harvests were affected by natural calamities, and there was a cotton crop shortfall. To overcome 1972 deficiencies, China imported some $1 billion worth of wheat, corn, soybeans and cotton during 1973, about half from the U.S.

With some 80 percent of the country's population still living in rural areas, agricultural developments have a tremendous influence on the overall economy. Since the early 1960s, China has followed a policy of "agriculture first." This policy, together with generally favorable climatic conditions, produced an average annual agricultural output increase of 3.4 percent during 1965-71, compared with 1.2 percent during 1957-65.

Poor crops in 1972 and only slight improvement in 1973 emphasize the need to develop agriculture further. Some economists, viewing the rapid growth of inputs such as fertilizer and equipment for the farm sector, predict that China is on the verge of a major expansion in agriculture. Skeptics believe, however, that China can never catch up in agriculture without utilizing direct incentives for the farmers.

Priorities for Development. The "agriculture first" policy will continue, but it should not be taken too literally. High priority is still being given to industrial development, especially machine-building, chemicals, and electronics. In 1972 the leading industrial sectors showed production gains as follows: pig iron, 12 percent; rolled steel, 10 percent; mining equipment, over 35 percent; tractors, 10 percent; and internal combustion engines, 25 percent. In the same year, China's steel output, which totaled 23 million metric tons in 1972, ranked seventh in the world.

The continuing efforts toward decentralization of economic management should prove to be beneficial for future growth. Efforts to build up local industry are based not only upon a desire to provide jobs in each locality, but also on a desire to disperse industry in case of military attack.

Despite a poor 1972 harvest, an only slightly better one in 1973, and the overall slowing down of industrial growth rates, China seems to be in the early stages of a new expansion. During 1971-75, agricultural output should increase 2.5 to 3.5 percent annually and the industrial growth rate will probably range between 8 and 12 percent. This would result in a real GNP increase of 5.5 to 7.5 percent annually.

Chinese Self-Reliance. A lot has been said and written about Chinese self-reliance and Peking's disinclination to become dependent on an outside power, with the Soviet experience cited as the prime example. But most serious analyses conclude that external participation in China's economic development is not only desirable, but that it will have the stabilizing political impact that is needed for China to develop.

The leaders of the free world believe that long-term, low-interest loans and technological assistance are essential if China is to develop as a profitable source of trade. But do these statesmen perceive the importance which such economic assistance has for the stability of the Peking government? William H. Whitson, the RAND Corporation China specialist, who has done some of the best work in portraying political influence in China's economy and foreign trade, developed this theme in a recent monograph.[1]

If foreign policy makers do demonstrate the vision and the will, their governments will certainly have the resources for extending to China the necessary long-term loans and technology which it can use to sustain the central regime's image of power not only abroad, but most importantly, at home.

It is not certain that such assistance will keep within reasonable limits the results of inevitable future power struggles, particularly those which will follow Mao's and Chou's departure from the scene, but without such assistance China's economic growth and the influence of the central regime over regional adversaries may falter, and the chances for a weakened central government will be greatly increased. This could lead to a replay of the tragic drama of the 1920s in China and East Asia.

Whitson wrote:

> From the viewpoint of foreign government and business strategists, trade and technology transfer from the advanced economies may become a crucial ingredient in persuading or coercing Chou's aging allies and adversaries at the regional level, their representatives at the center and their youthful successors.

---

[1] William W. Whitson, *The Succession Question in China: Problems and Prospects for the 1970s*, privately printed and distributed by Whitson, 1973.

Time is growing short, obviously. The pace of personnel changes must therefore be expected to remain brisk as Chou carries out the last great political campaign of his career, utilizing all along the thoughts of Chairman Mao.[2]

David Rockefeller, the chairman of the board of the Chase Manhattan Bank, who visited China in 1973, provided a slightly different perspective.[3] Rockefeller said that he feared that too often the true significance and potential of our new relationship with China has been obscured by the novelty of it all—pandas, ping-pong, elaborate dinners, travel in a country that has been closed and alien for so long. He said that when one considers the profound differences in our cultural heritages and our social and economic systems, it can be realized how long and difficult the task of accommodation will be. Rockefeller said: "The social experiment in China under Chairman Mao's leadership is one of the most important and successful in human history. How extensively China opens up and how the world interprets and reacts to the social innovations and life styles she has developed is certain to have a profound impact on the future of many nations." [4] It is in the broad context suggested by Rockefeller that the real significance of the future of Sino-American trade can be fully imagined.[5]

Sino-American Trade: A Brief Perspective

In 1937 an American businessman named Carl Crowe wrote a book, entitled *400 Million Customers,* about the potential of mainland China as a market for American goods and services. The concept captured the imagination of many businessmen and the book went through eleven printings. But for all his drum-beating, Crowe proved that the United States was a better market for "promise 'em anything" literature than was China a market for American goods.

---

[2] Ibid.

[3] *New York Times,* 10 August 1973, p. 31.

[4] Ibid.

[5] Rather than go into greater detail here, the authors recommend that the reader refer to three basic volumes for further reading and continuing reference: *Mainland China in the World Economy*, Report of the Joint Economic Committee, U.S. Congress (Washington, D.C.: Government Printing Office, 1967); *People's Republic of China: An Economic Assessment,* a compendium of papers submitted to the Joint Economic Committee, U.S. Congress (Washington, D.C.: Government Printing Office, 1972); Yuan-li Wu, ed., *China: A Handbook* (New York: Praeger Publishers, 1973).

The China market that Crowe envisioned never materialized. But this rather severe fact of history has never prevented Americans from giving it a try. The possibility of selling "oil for the lamps of China" is no less intoxicating today than in 1937.

Many American importers and exporters today see in China the ultimate commercial opportunity. In his recent book, John Paton Davies, Jr., gives an enlightening and entertaining account of the nineteenth century intrusion of Western traders, including Americans, into China.[6] He records the rampant enthusiasm of the mercantile spirit, dazzled by China trade prospects. The enormous Chinese population was seen by many then—and still is—as an inexhaustible market of eager buyers.

Davies wrote that the textile manufacturers of Great Britain, for example, "were excited by the thought of adding an inch to every China-man's gown" and that "American tobacco growers were elated by a vision of displacing opium with chewing tobacco, the mouth-watering prospect of four hundred million quids a day."

New Era in China Trade. The Shanghai Joint Communiqué issued at the conclusion of President Nixon's visit in February 1972 stated: "Both sides view bilateral trade as another area from which mutual benefit can be derived, and agreed that economic relations based on equality and mutual benefit are in the interest of the peoples of the two countries. They agreed to facilitate the progressive development of trade between their two countries."

The expression "equality and mutual benefit" warrants special attention because, although a similar thought is often expressed in U.S. trade policy and East European Communist statements, the particular phraseology is vintage Chinese. The words "equality and mutual benefit" occur in Chairman Mao's writings and in virtually all Chinese pronouncements regarding external political and economic relations.

Following the joint communiqué, the Chinese had another opportunity to express themselves on the matter of trade. At a meeting of the United Nations Conference on Trade and Development (UNCTAD) at Santiago, Chile, in April 1972, Chinese Vice Minister of Trade Chou Hua-min told the delegates:

> In international economic and trade relations, the United
> States has all along pursued a policy of expansion and plunder

---

[6] John Paton Davies, Jr., *Dragon by the Tail* (New York: W. W. Norton and Co., 1972), p. 48.

and of profiteering at the expense of other countries. . . . For over a century, the imperialist powers . . . divided China into their spheres of influence, interfered in China's internal affairs, backed the reactionary authorities, subjected the Chinese people's revolutionary struggle to bloody suppression, engineered civil wars among warlords, controlled China's customs, shipping and insurance, manipulated China's financial and monetary affairs and extorted privileges of running mines and factories, building railways, inland navigation, etc. They flagrantly plundered China's resources, fleeced the Chinese people, and seriously disrupted the national economy of old China.

The vice minister concluded with the view that economic and trade relations should be governed by the five principles of mutual respect for territorial integrity and national sovereignty, mutual nonaggression, noninterference in each other's internal affairs, peaceful coexistence, and equality and mutual benefit.

It is safe to say that a new era in China trade has arrived and, significantly, it has been brought about as a direct result of the beginning of Sino-American trade. The most visible sign of this change is now seen at the twice-yearly Chinese Export Commodities Fair. The past practice of a clubby group of "old China hands" turning up every spring and autumn in Canton to sign trade deals which offered high profitability is over.

Since 1972, a much more business-like attitude has been adopted by the Chinese. Now that they are quoting prices "at the world market levels," as Chinese officials repeatedly say, China is learning about foreign markets in a way it never has before. There are clear indications that Peking wants its foreign trade to grow at a rate of at least 10 percent per year. Two-way trade in 1973 totaled over $8 billion, compared with a little more than $5 billion in 1972.

To sustain this kind of growth, the Chinese are striving to make their export products more attractive and suitable for foreign markets; China's trade officials have ordered market surveys of Canada, the U.S., and Europe. The implications are far-reaching: more than ever before the Chinese are taking seriously foreign businessmen's requests on such things as styling, labeling, and packaging to make Chinese goods more acceptable.

Peking must increase its exports if it is to continue buying complete plants and other high-technology items which it requires. The new practice of arranging deferred payment for high-cost imports such as complete plants is another indication of the shifting Chinese attitude.

United States trade with China in 1973 increased tenfold from the 1972 level. Exports to China totaled $689.1 million, while imports from China totaled $64 million, according to the U.S. Department of Commerce.

The thaw in political relations between the two nations went hand in hand with economic conditions in China—the poor Chinese grain harvest in 1972 and the new Chinese desire to acquire Western technology were certainly powerful considerations in Peking's thinking.

Chinese and American leaders seem prepared to let their economic relations move forward more or less independent of political issues. This is in contrast to Soviet-American relations where leaders on both sides intertwine trade discussions with political talks. President Nixon and Secretary of State Kissinger have used economics as a weapon in dealing with the Soviets. U.S. government officials acknowledge, for example, that they delayed the wheat deal in 1972 pending Soviet agreement on the strategic nuclear arms treaty. The President and Kissinger are said to believe that a prime reason the Kremlin wants detente to work is the hope of gaining access to American trade, technology, and credits.

Similarly, China has used the lure of profits in its contacts with Japan. Peking held up an airline agreement with Japan until Japan cancelled its airline pact with Taiwan.

But in American-Chinese relations, both sides have tended to treat political issues apart from the development of overall economic considerations. Peking seems interested in detente with Washington in order to have a friend against the Soviets. Washington is said to be interested in better relations with Peking primarily in order to have another lever against the U.S.S.R.

China's worldwide trade went from $4.7 billion in 1971 to $5.8 billion in 1972 and to more than $8 billion in 1973. This represents about 4 percent of China's GNP, or about the same proportion as in the U.S.S.R.

Three-quarters of the $689.1 million of U.S. exports to China in 1973 were in agricultural products—wheat, corn, cotton and soybeans. Since the 1972 Chinese grain harvest was poor, China turned to America for farm products as well as industrial products and advanced technology. The largest single transaction was the sale of ten Boeing 707s for $125 million.

12

Two-thirds of China's exports to the United States were in the form of primary products—silk and hog bristles for toothbrushes and paint brushes. China also exported antiques, food specialties and light manufactured goods such as rugs.

The most pressing problem in Sino-American trade relations is the heavy deficit that China is running. Up to now, China has met this situation by using its trade surplus with trading partners such as Singapore and Hong Kong to offset this deficit. China's overall imports and exports appear to be in balance but this cannot last indefinitely because of China's desire for increased imports.

Obstacles to Increased Chinese Exports. China is expected to move to increase its exports to the U.S., but there are some obstacles. There are serious legal problems, including private American claims dating back twenty-five years against Chinese expropriation of property totaling $197 million. This means that China cannot hold a trade fair or open bank accounts in the United States without the risk of these claimants attaching Chinese goods and money.

Chinese government funds in American banks totaling about $75 million have been blocked since 1950. Negotiations are under way to settle the private American claims and to unblock China's bank accounts.

There is the problem of most-favored-nation status. U.S. duty on Chinese imports would be reduced by about 15 percent if this non-discriminatory status were conferred. And Washington may seek reciprocity—for example, facilities for businessmen, shipping arrangements and port openings.

Then there is the problem for China of learning how to make its products salable in Western markets. This means finding out about competitive pricing, labeling, and conformity to regulations such as those imposed by the U.S. Food and Drug Administration.

On the positive side, near the end of 1973 a contract was signed which may set the pattern for Sino-American cooperation in the next two decades. The M. W. Kellogg Company, a division of Pullman, Inc., announced in November that it had been awarded five contracts from China for the construction of large-scale ammonia plants valued at a total of $130 million.[7] Along with three similar contracts worth

---

[7] *New York Times*, 28 November 1973.

$70 million, the contracts represent the largest orders in the industrial sector ever placed by China with an American company.

Each contract called for the design, engineering, and supply of materials and equipment for plants to be constructed in China, each to produce 1,000 metric tons of ammonia per day. All equipment and materials will be purchased in the United States, and export licenses have been obtained. Kellogg will provide advisory services during the construction and start of all the units. The target date for completion of the first unit is 1976 and the other units will be completed at three-month intervals.

In addition to the eight plants, Kellogg also obtained joint contracts for two other similar ammonia plants. It will supply information to the Toyo Engineering Corporation of Japan, which will engineer facilities using the Kellogg design.

A Kellogg Dutch affiliate has been awarded contracts for eight synthetic fertilizer plants, each with a capacity of 1,620 metric tons of urea a day, making them the largest such plants in the world. The total value of the eight plants is about $90 million.

China's Oil Reserves. China's crude oil reserves in 1971 amounted to 2,729 billion tons, equal to 3.27 percent of the world's reserves,[8] thus placing China twelfth in the world in proven oil reserves. The above data omit any possible offshore oil reserves and are based on fragmentary information. The Chinese seem convinced that they have vast oil and gas reserves. They are buying very sophisticated equipment and machinery for oil and gas exploration, extraction, and refining. Meanwhile the P.R.C. is self-sufficient in refined products including aviation fuel.

If China's reserves are even a fraction of what is claimed, the authors believe that in a matter of a few years China will be in a position to use her earnings from oil and gas to pay for imports of technology and other foreign goods. In fact, oil could become China's leading earner of foreign exchange.[9] Graham Metson, trade officer for the People's Re-

---

[8] *Oil and Gas Journal*, 13 December 1971.

[9] For an excellent analysis of China's oil prospects, see Nicholas Ludlow, "China's Oil," *U.S.-China Business Review*, vol. 1, no. 1 (January-February 1974), published by the National Council on U.S.-China Trade. Together with other aspects of the question, Ludlow discusses the complicated question of territorial waters along Asia's rim and the offshore oil deposits beneath these waters. The 19 January 1974 incident in which Chinese MiGs attacked South Vietnamese vessels in the

public of China, Bureau of East Asian and Pacific Affairs, U.S. State Department, confirmed that the Chinese are inquiring all over the world about the various types of oil well equipment.

Paracel Islands area is directly related to China's oil intentions, Ludlow asserts. The article also suggests the possibility that oil could be Peking's wedge toward Taiwan: "Exports of China's oil to Taiwan would create a link Peking has been seeking to forge that would be more than symbolic." Ludlow says that mainland China's oil, at cheap prices, could someday fuel Taiwan's industries after a political settlement were reached and notes that "Some U.S. firms are known to be thinking in those terms."

3
Factors Affecting Trade

Politics in Command

The People's Republic of China is better organized today and proceeding on its course of nation-building with more self-confidence than at any time since its founding in 1949. But can the tranquility and calm—compared to the turmoil of the Cultural Revolution, for example—continue? What happens when Mao and Chou En-lai die? Will the competition between the left and right, between the so-called "two lines," shift from abstract debates to bloody struggles for power? How can the United States commit itself to expanded trade with a country which is seemingly so unpredictable and even unstable?

The "Two Lines" Debate. There is in China a lively debate over Mao's "revolutionary foreign policy," as the new detente with the West in general and the U.S. in particular is called.[1] This debate is known as the "two lines." One hard, revolutionary line is espoused by a group under the leadership of Wang Hung-wen, which views the new ties with

---

[1] There are several good current discussions of internal politics in the P.R.C. For events through mid-1973, see Henry S. Bradsher, "China: The Radical Offensive," *Asian Survey*, November 1973, pp. 989-1009. The beginnings of the current campaign criticizing the late Lin Piao and Confucius are explored astutely and with appropriate caution by Stanley Karnow in "Winds of Change in Mao's China," *Washington Post*, 3 March 1974, and by Robert Keatley in "China's Well Orchestrated Disorder" in *Wall Street Journal*, 7 March 1974. The bottom line of their assessments is that, as of spring 1974, the campaign showed no signs of becoming as violent or turbulent as the Cultural Revolution. Keatley quotes analysts as believing the "so-called 'pragmatists' led by Premier Chou En-lai will retain state power, and with the Chairman's [Mao Tse-tung] blessing. And they expect no changes in Chinese foreign policy—most particularly no cooling of the friendly relationship between Washington and Peking."

the capitalist world with great suspicion and would prefer to concentrate on domestic affairs and continue a hostile policy toward the U.S. in particular. Wang is under fifty and joined the top leadership recently after a very rapid climb to power. The moderates, under Chou, are pragmatic and see advantages for China in expanded relations with the free world. The Ministries of Foreign Affairs and of Foreign Trade are almost wholly staffed with Chou men and quite obviously the moderates have made a good deal of progress, as the very existence of detente indicates. As in all Communist countries the visible part of the struggle is waged in the press, and during late 1973 and early 1974 there were lively exchanges of editorials and articles.[2] Chinese officials have gone to great pains to give an impression that the debate is not serious and that nothing will be permitted to disturb trade. Mao has said that contention between the "two lines" is a good thing. As long as Mao remains in power we believe that nothing will be allowed to disrupt trade.

Stripped of Communist terminology, the key Chinese concern has been a search for the proper route to modernizing a backward nation. It is the clash of factions holding differing views on this basic question— plus the naked striving for power by individual personalities—that comprises the political power game in the P.R.C. today.

The pivotal questions for China—they were present to a degree even before communism arrived—are: How are we to modernize? Which elements of the past are supportive of modernity? What features of Western civilization—West European, Russian, or American—must China accept in order to be able to respond effectively to the West? How much of China's heritage can be preserved?

In essence, the question is one of finding a path to modernization which will preserve national pride. Within the ruling hierarchy, one group has long advocated adherence to the Soviet model. Many Chinese Communists felt that China could follow the Soviet path without becoming a "little brother."

Michael Oskenberg, associate professor of political science at Columbia University, notes that "the actual experience of importing Soviet governmental forms soon made the Chinese aware that the Soviet model was culture-bound."[3] Oskenberg believes that those in China

---

[2] For Peking's official version of the developing campaign against Lin Piao and Confucius, see *Peking Review*, especially no. 5 (1 February 1974); no. 6 (8 February 1974); no. 7 (15 February 1974); and no. 8 (22 February 1974).

[3] *Problems of Communism*, March-April 1974, p. 9.

who now want to borrow from the West—having turned their backs on the Soviet Union—"suffer from their cosmopolitanism" in the eyes of many Chinese.

The modernizers—like Chou En-lai—advocate sophisticated notions of specialization and complex organization which arouse hostility in the Chinese cultural context, and their political opponents have sought to capitalize on this hostility. China's opening to the West has not paid the dividends that would make the policy popular with some Chinese leaders (for example, Taiwan has not been recovered), and the visits by Westerners and purchase of Western—notably American—technology has brought into question once again the matter of Chinese dependence on outsiders.

What we are witnessing is ancient China, bound by traditions of thousands of years now overlaid with the veneer of communism, moving slowly toward modernization. Each step of the way is being marked by debate and political struggle over which is the best way to proceed.

The Succession Problem. The day of reckoning will come when Mao dies or becomes incapacitated. There are a number of potential successors. Far ahead of the rest is Chou; as premier he wields a great deal of power which sets him apart from the other candidates. But at seventy-five, he cannot expect to survive Mao by many years. Wang, the radical mentioned earlier, is rated number three in party listings, but has no power base of his own and may be there as a representative of "the young." Li Teh-sheng, in his late fifties, appears to be running the armed forces, and is ranked fourth.[4] Chang Chun-chiao, number five, is prominent in party affairs. Mao's wife, Chiang Ching, has received a good deal of publicity, but recently slipped from third to tenth in party rankings.

While virtually no hard information is available, it is possible that rule by committee will emerge in China after Mao's and Chou's deaths, as happened in the U.S.S.R. after Stalin, and again after Khrushchev, died. Whether a Khrushchev will emerge is impossible to tell.

For the long term we believe that China will tend to increase its foreign trade. Whether as a spur to development and modernization or

---

[4] In a New Year's 1974 reshuffle of military commanders, Li Teh-sheng was shifted to the Shenyang command, which fronts on a key section of the Sino-Soviet border. Some commanders who were shifted from that area to other posts were believed to be among those advocating a less rigid Peking posture toward Moscow.

as a means to make up for failures in production, the P.R.C. will need to trade aggressively. This is particularly true in agriculture.

The People-Food Equation

Many analysts have attempted to explain the relative speed and depth of the Peking-Washington rapprochement solely in strategic military terms. More than 1 million Soviet soldiers along China's borders seemed reason enough to motivate the Peking leadership to send Chinese emissaries in search of a powerful friend who could balance the threat from Moscow.

The relationship with the Soviet Union, especially the military threat, is undoubtedly a major concern to Peking. But through bitter experience, the Chinese have learned that outside friends are useful and necessary on grounds other than those of military strategy.

At this point, one of China's pressing needs is a guaranteed food supply. The need for a standby food source was unquestionably an important consideration leading to the detente with the United States. It is an intriguing experience to be reminded by a Chinese Foreign Ministry official that the United States exports two-thirds of its wheat, half its soybeans, one-fourth of its feed grains, half of its cattle hides, two-thirds of its rice, and one-third of its cotton.

So while the Chinese are aiming at self-sufficiency in agriculture, it is comforting for them to know they may now in emergencies turn to the United States for food.

Population: A Basic Dimension. Population is not frequently mentioned in analyses of a nation's foreign trade performance and potential, but in China's case it is an issue that must be confronted. Population is perhaps the basic dimension of human society; it is the measure of human assets and liabilities.

Because China's basic problem is still the management of the people-food equation, we believe more free world attention should be given to China's efforts to solve this problem. If the Chinese are successful, they will not only have made a major contribution to the rest of the world, but they will have increased their potential in many areas—including foreign trade.

The study of population in China is hampered by the fact that no accurate census has ever been taken. Not even Peking knows for certain how many persons live inside the boundaries of the P.R.C. The best estimates range between 800 and 900 million with a growth rate of about 2 percent. The population of the world in 1973 was about 3.7 billion and will increase to at least 6.5 billion and possibly more than 7 billion by the year 2000, of which one-quarter will be Chinese.

Except for the three disaster years of 1959-61, China has been able to feed its enormous population, no small accomplishment. Birth control programs and new stress on agricultural technology have been the main lines of approach to the challenge.

The agricultural investment strategy adopted following the Great Leap Forward included an increased use of chemical fertilizers, more pumps for water control, increased production of tractors, improved transportation and an emphasis on the use of these resources on the high-yield rice land of south China.

According to an analysis by John S. Aird, a U.S. government census expert, China's birth control programs have thus far had little effect on the country's demographic rates. Also, no matter how successful are China's attempts at fertility reduction they would probably have little effect on the size of the population over the next twenty years. Aird's four population models show projections for 1990 that range only between 1.319 and 1.330 billion.[5]

The model projections suggest that, barring catastrophe or spectacular changes in contraceptive technology and in the means of political coercion, even the most successful family limitation effort is not likely to have much effect "until mortality has completed its transition to the lower levels characteristic of developed countries." [6] On the other hand, the failure to make significant progress in family limitation while continuing to reduce the mortality levels can only increase the rate of population growth. Taking into account the experiences of the three birth control campaigns, Aird sees no reason to expect any great change in China's demographic prospects in the immediate future.

The general conclusion of Aird and other experts is that new investment will permit agriculture to keep pace with population, but that agriculture will provide no extra margin for stepped-up economic growth.

---

[5] *People's Republic of China: An Economic Assessment*, p. 327.
[6] Ibid., p. 331.

Progress in Agriculture. Alva Lewis Erisman, an agricultural economist, has analyzed the impact of Peking's new high-investment-in-agriculture policy.[7] He finds that "miracle increases" are not likely to be achieved for the balance of the current Five-Year Plan (1971-75). Although China has improved its agricultural sector since 1962, it lacks much of the institutional infrastructure and scientific competence necessary for a green revolution.

Erisman wrote: "The gains of the next few years will be obtained from the gradual extension of high-yield acreage, the increase in supplies of both high-grade and low-grade fertilizers, and the steady improvement of seed varieties." These gains probably will be sufficient to maintain per capita food supplies, but not enough to provide large extra quantities of raw materials for industry or export.

Erisman went on to say that

> A run of bad luck in weather or a retreat from the per-
> missive policy toward private activity in the countryside would
> reduce these gains. Shortcomings in domestic agricultural
> technology will increasingly constrain the advance of the agri-
> cultural sector. By picking up the pieces and starting anew on
> a basic agricultural research program, Peking could substan-
> tially improve long-term prospects.[8]

Another analysis of Chinese agriculture was presented at a November 1973 meeting of the Food and Agriculture Organization (FAO). According to the FAO report, based on estimates, 78 percent of the cropland in the P.R.C. is now irrigated, compared with only 16 percent in 1952. In the off-season an estimated 25 billion man-days are employed annually in an effort to make China completely immune from floods and droughts—an objective not yet reached.

Nevertheless, the report states that

> China's agriculture is not moving as fast as the government
> desires. The overall levels of production are not yet high
> enough. In many places development is not balanced, and
> quality often leaves much to be desired. Many farm units
> are still not fulfilling their targets and, in spite of a great deal
> of sustained capital construction, China's agriculture is not yet
> fully protected against natural calamities. There are still
> threats of drought, waterlogging, floods and pests. The irriga-
> tion facilities in the hill areas are not yet sufficient. The extent

---

[7] Ibid., pp. 142-143.
[8] Ibid.

and quality of agricultural training and extension are not yet satisfactory.[9]

The Implications of Success. What are some of the implications of a Chinese solution of the people-food problem? First of all, China has or will soon have more experience—at least quantitatively and perhaps qualitatively—in population control policy and practice than any other developing nation in the world. Peking, through its representatives at the United Nations, has shown a willingness to pass on to other nations of the world some of its expertise and to learn from the experience of others.

China's self-financing of regional population centers, decentralization of decision making to the lowest level, high degree of flexibility in planning, emphasis on training of cadres, introduction of persuasive methods to develop peasant motivation, and—above all—efficient organization are models from which the international community can benefit. Organizational forms that have proved successful in one type of society may well be adjusted to other types. These need not necessarily conflict with ideological requirements. This would be particularly true for the mixed type of society that some developing countries have adopted.

As for foreign trade, should China get to the point where its population growth is in balance with its agricultural production and its technology is sufficient to free more farmers for factory jobs, the results would be dramatic. This is not to say that China will ever be a consumer market for foreign goods like Coca-Cola and hairspray. But if China gets involved in the world market, and its citizens begin producing significantly more products than they consume, China's share of world commerce could someday be staggering indeed, exceeding the most optimistic projections of today.

Eagle, Dragon and Bear

In an earlier book in this series, Robert A. Scalapino suggested that "little time need be spent in contemplating this possibility" of a Peking-Washington alliance.[10] Recent events, Scalapino said, have shown that

---

[9] Food and Agriculture Organization (FAO), *Report of the Rome Meeting,* November 1973.

[10] Robert A. Scalapino, *Asia and the Major Powers* (Washington, D.C.: American Enterprise Institute-Hoover Institution, 1972), p. 28.

two nations holding as radically different values and policies as China and the United States can reach an improved level of communication and even some degree of accommodation when mutual self-interest warrants it. "This type of development we label 'normalization,' " said Scalapino. "There is a vast difference, however, between normalization of relations and an alliance." [11]

Without getting into semantic shadings, it strikes us that "alliances" in the accepted sense of the word may be increasingly obsolete in the future. Practically speaking, superpowers or near-superpowers cannot afford to be linked too closely with another big power to the exclusion of others.

Although from the vantage point of 1972 Scalapino believed "a Sino-American alliance has no raison d'être, economically, politically or in terms of mutual security interests," [12] it can be said that from the perspective of 1974, a Sino-American "connection" makes eminent sense economically, politically and in terms of mutual security.

Political and Diplomatic Value of the Detente. The Sino-American normalization is a fact of great political and diplomatic value to both sides. President Nixon, under threat of impeachment, has described the detente with China as one of the great achievements of his administration. Meanwhile, the solid U.S. relationship with China affords Washington some intriguing diplomatic leverage with Moscow.

Mao and Chou apparently have reasons of their own for demonstrating the solidity of their American ties. "The implicit Sino-American alliance which the Mao-Chou group has made with the Nixon administration is essential, Peking appears to believe, to diminish the chances of a Soviet attack," according to an editorial in the *Washington Post*.[13] We suspect that Nixon would like to switch official relations from Taipei to Peking before the end of his present term in 1976.

The U.S., the P.R.C., and the U.S.S.R. form a triangle of power which will be of great significance for the world in the next quarter-century.[14] It would be a mistake to put too much emphasis on this or

---

[11] Ibid.

[12] Ibid.

[13] *Washington Post*, 26 November 1973, p. C6.

[14] For a detailed discussion of this subject, see *The Great Power Triangle*, compiled by the Subcommittee on National Security and International Operations of the Committee on Government Operations, U.S. Senate. The compiled papers include opinions by Michael Tatu, correspondent for *Le Monde*, writing for the

24

that geometric shape being "the" most important format for the coming two decades. Nevertheless, we attach primary importance to the balance of power within the triangle of United States-China-Soviet Union and to a slightly lesser extent, the balance of power within a hexagon of the United States-China-Soviet Union-Japan-Europe-Arab oil-producing states.[15]

Although China disclaims at every opportunity her desire to be a superpower, the great power triangle is an emerging reality. Provided the U.S.S.R. does not become sufficiently alarmed at China's increased nuclear strength to attempt a preemptive strike, it appears that the three powers will reach a mutual balance of force such as the U.S. and the U.S.S.R. have had for the past quarter of a century.

The Importance of Economic Power. Under this assumption, economic power will be the main factor in world power terms for the remainder of this century, and the areas of monetary relationships and food and energy supply will become more and more significant. This is the reason that the Arab oil-producing states rate inclusion in our power "hexagon."

The Sino-American tie is one of convenience for both sides, enhancing their separate but parallel rivalries with the Soviet Union. Note that China has all but given sanction to continued strong American positions around the world. This has even caused China to look ridiculous in the eyes of some for the no-vote, no-veto stand Peking took on the Middle East question at the United Nations in the autumn of 1973.

Peking raised no objections to Kissinger's comments while in Peking publicizing U.S. Middle East initiatives, including the possibility of an offer of a permanent U.S. security guarantee to Israel. Ordinarily China would object to an offer of that type as an imperialist device to legalize American hegemony or intervention. Such are China's apprehensions about the Soviet Union, however, that in this frame of reference it is willing to set ideology and reflex rhetoric aside even at the risk of appearing inconsistent in the eyes of some Third World nations.

Atlantic Institute, 1970; Richard Moorsteen and Morton Abramowitz, RAND Corporation and Institute of Strategic Studies, respectively; G. F. Hudson, fellow emeritus, St. Anthony's College, Oxford; and Zbigniew Brzezinski, director, Research Institute on Communist Affairs, Columbia University.

[15] For a recent comprehensive analysis of this subject, see Robert A. Scalapino, "China and the Balance of Power," *Foreign Affairs*, January 1974, pp. 349-385.

The Sino-Soviet Dispute. In the short term, the Sino-Soviet dispute remains the most serious international situation in the world today. Because it directly involves two of the three members of the great power triangle there is much greater danger of a nuclear holocaust developing there than in the Middle East.

A menacing Soviet military force stands along China's border, and Peking has responded by building up its own nuclear arsenal, constructing an impressive network of underground shelters, continually warning the Chinese population to expect an attack at any time, and reaching for more friendly links to Japan, Europe, and the United States.[16]

Moscow's position appears to be one of waiting to see if there will be opportunities for advantage in the succession to Mao-Chou which cannot be far off. This helps explain the Soviet Union's refusal to negotiate with more speed and enthusiasm on the key border issue, even though China's recent offers on the controversy have been reasonable enough.

Future Developments. We foresee world developments for the next quarter-century as follows:

1. Sino-American ties will continue to be strong, allowing for some ups and downs, especially in economic development and trade relations. The pace of the growth of the relationship—especially in terms of trade, travel and tourism—will be greatly accelerated when formal diplomatic ties are established.

---

[16] For the most authoritative recent statement on China's progress in developing an ICBM and China's nuclear capability compared to that of the U.S. and the U.S.S.R., see "Report of the Secretary of Defense James R. Schlesinger to the Congress on the FY 1975 Budget and the FY 1975-79 Defense Program," published on 4 March 1974. Near the beginning of his report Schlesinger describes the situation facing the United States: "A policy requiring us to maintain our military strength and alliances while we are actively pursuing detente with the Soviet Union and the People's Republic of China may appear to some as incongruous. We have a long tradition in this country of arming with great haste when war comes upon us, and disarming with even greater haste when the war is over; and we have tended, often, to view our relations with other nations in terms of absolutes—friend or foe, ally or adversary, cold war or detente. Unfortunately, the real world is more complicated."

Schlesinger also notes that the P.R.C. land-based ballistic missile program is progressing "slowly but steadily." And he added: "Most important from the U.S. point of view is the continuing development of the ICBM, which was flight tested again in 1973. We remain convinced that the P.R.C. will pursue that program to a successful conclusion and achieve an ICBM capability before the end of this decade."

26

2. Continued Moscow-Washington economic ties based on real Soviet requirements for U.S. exports, together with U.S. diplomatic efforts, will diffuse the threat of a Sino-Soviet war.

3. A tense period following the passing of Mao Tse-tung and Chou En-lai will be followed by increasingly improved relations between Moscow and Peking. Peking will not allow trade with the U.S.S.R. to reach the levels of trade with the United States (which we believe will be China's best trading partner before 1980) or Japan.

4. Japan will play an important role in the world balance of power by trading and participating in joint economic ventures with both the Soviet Union and China, while continuing to maintain strong economic and investment ties to the U.S. Japan's role in the future is especially intriguing.[17] If Japan's industrial strength were to be aligned with any one member of the three great powers, it could cause a marked imbalance. Most long-range speculation on this question revolves around a possible China-Japan merger or alliance, strong in both industry and manpower.

5. The Arab oil-producing states will be allowed to invest in the U.S., Japanese, and European economies to the extent of guaranteeing against future oil boycotts. China will become a significant supplier of oil to Asia, especially Japan.

It is against this backdrop of stability and peace—secured essentially by the U.S.-U.S.S.R. nuclear standoff—in the coming two decades among members of the great power triangle that we forecast Sino-American trade and development relationships to move far beyond the limits presently forecast by those who attach too much weight to past performance instead of future possibilities.

---

[17] The authors' premise that, in the future, power in Asia will be defined in economic terms is not universally shared. Japan's difficult position during the Arab oil embargo caused some analysts to suggest that Japanese rearmament might be a result. The question is explored in depth in John K. Emmerson and Leonard A. Humphreys, *Will Japan Rearm?* (Washington, D.C.: American Enterprise Institute-Hoover Institution, 1973). Among those who tend to believe Japan will indeed rearm because its survival rests in the hands of others is military affairs analyst John J. O'Malley. Writing in the *San Diego Union*, 4 March 1973, O'Malley said: "It is not hard to perceive the inevitability of Japan's rearmament. When this happens there will be the sobering spectacle of three great military powers looking hard at one another in that corner of the Pacific—Japan, China and Soviet Russia. These are countries whose mutual mistrust is legendary—and this certainly is not the stuff of which peace and tranquility are made."

4
The Machinery of Trade

P.R.C. Administrative Structure

The scene is Chicago in the year 1980. The U.S. secretary of commerce and the minister of foreign trade of the People's Republic of China jointly snip a ribbon opening the "biggest yet" China Products Trade Exhibition in the United States. Among those applauding politely are the Chicago office manager of the Bank of China (a Chinese educated at Harvard in the 1930s) and his American counterpart who has flown home from Peking for the occasion.

The exhibits include compact Shanghai family sedans with the latest emission-control equipment and priced competitively with Datsuns and Toyotas, Chinese-made blue jeans, ladies' pants-suits, garden tractors, and radios. A special booth is staffed with smiling Chinese airline hostesses passing out brochures advertising "Air China Flights, San Francisco to Shanghai" and "20-day Adventure Tours to Peking, Tientsin, Wuhan and Tibet."

The National Council for U.S.-China Trade is already planning for visits by Peking trade officials as a prelude to the first American trade exhibitions in China and the first Chinese exhibitions in the United States.

Each year the P.R.C. participates in trade fairs and exhibitions in a number of foreign countries and also hosts exhibitions in China, usually in Peking but sometimes in Shanghai or Tientsin. There were nine such exhibitions in China in 1972 and a dozen in 1973. Peking's excellent exhibition facilities are already booked through 1974.

29

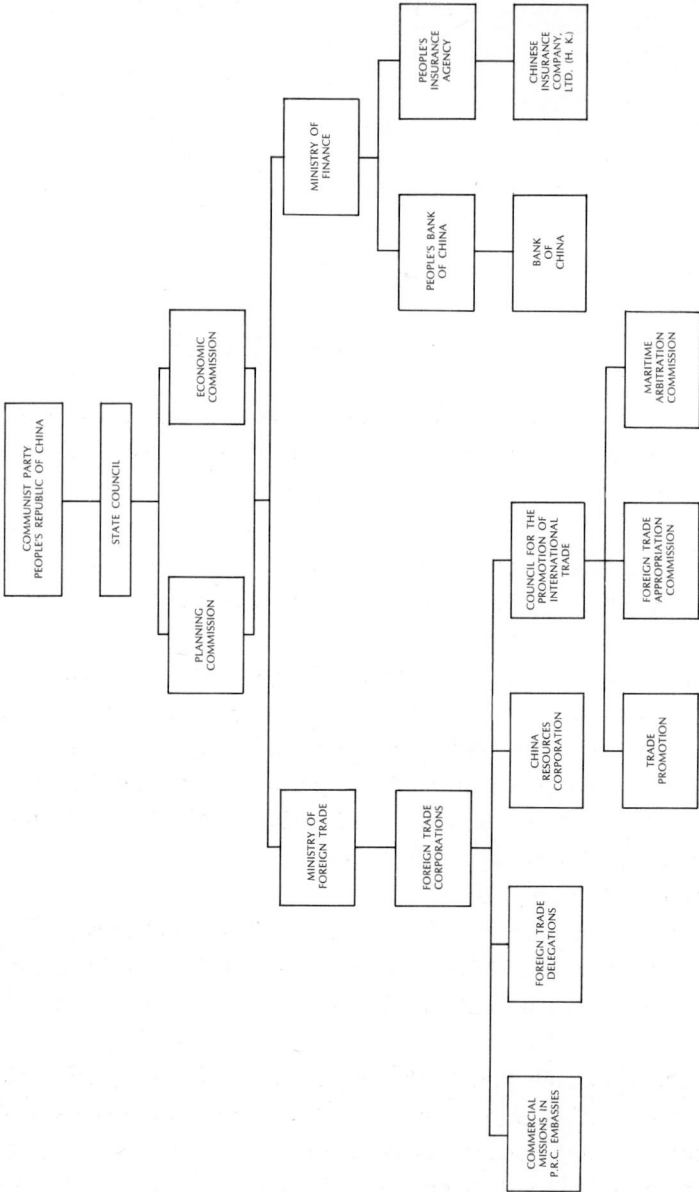

COMMUNIST PARTY
PEOPLE'S REPUBLIC OF CHINA

STATE COUNCIL

ECONOMIC COMMISSION

PLANNING COMMISSION

MINISTRY OF FINANCE

PEOPLE'S INSURANCE AGENCY

CHINESE INSURANCE COMPANY, LTD. (H. K.)

PEOPLE'S BANK OF CHINA

BANK OF CHINA

MINISTRY OF FOREIGN TRADE

FOREIGN TRADE CORPORATIONS

COUNCIL FOR THE PROMOTION OF INTERNATIONAL TRADE

CHINA RESOURCES CORPORATION

FOREIGN TRADE DELEGATIONS

COMMERCIAL MISSIONS IN P.R.C. EMBASSIES

MARITIME ARBITRATION COMMISSION

FOREIGN TRADE APPROPRIATION COMMISSION

TRADE PROMOTION

The State Trading Corporations. Exhibitions play a major role—as does the Canton Trade Fair—in the work of the Ministry of Foreign Trade. The ministry conducts foreign trade through a network of state trading corporations organized according to the commodities or services for which they are responsible. The state trading corporations have main offices in Peking with branch offices in industrial centers.[1]

The state trading corporations have the responsibility for negotiating and administering contracts for the purchase of goods and services according to the annual export-import plan. Although there has been some change in this practice lately, foreign firms rarely meet with the producers or end-users of the products which they are trading.

In addition to controlling these trading corporations, the Ministry of Foreign Trade maintains overseas personnel, such as commercial attachés at diplomatic posts, to provide liaison between foreign firms and the trading corporations; trade or purchasing offices like that in Berne, Switzerland, for Europe; and special missions to hold trade exhibitions, make special purchases or sales, and conduct market surveys.

The ministry has the additional responsibility of supervising the Customs Administration and the Commodity Inspection and Testing Bureau. It also collaborates with the People's Bank of China on an annual plan for commercial payments for P.R.C. purchases abroad. The bank forwards an overall foreign exchange plan to the State Council for approval.

Promotion of Trade. The Committee for the Promotion of International Trade (CPIT) promotes trade and provides for arbitration of commercial disputes, but is not strictly a government agency, according to the Chinese. It is in many respects like a national chamber of commerce. It works with state agencies and private trade associations in other countries. The CPIT runs Chinese trade exhibitions at home and overseas, is host to foreign trade delegations and exhibitions, manages business and familiarization trips for Chinese trade and production officials abroad, and serves as an informal liaison with foreign businessmen for the trading corporations. It is in charge of trademark registration. Its members include trade officials from several agencies, economists, and representatives of the workers.

The CPIT set up the Foreign Trade Arbitration Commission and the Maritime Arbitration Commission to settle disputes with foreign

---

[1] See Appendix C for a complete list of Chinese trading corporations.

31

importers and exporters. These institutions have been used sparingly because the Chinese traditionally prefer informal negotiation or mediation to formal arbitration of disputes, and this has worked out satisfactorily in most cases. The Chinese scrupulously follow the provisions of trade contracts and expect the same of foreign companies.

Main foreign trade guidelines, of course, originate at the very top—that means in consultations between Mao and Chou. They pass through the State Council, which is roughly the equivalent of the American presidential cabinet. Implementing foreign trade policies is the job of the minister of foreign trade.

New Minister of Foreign Trade. During the fall of 1973 the P.R.C. revealed the appointment of a new foreign trade boss in a traditionally low-key manner. A Hsinhua (New China) News Agency announcement of a commercial agreement with North Vietnam casually mentioned that Li Chiang, "Chinese Minister of Foreign Trade," had signed the agreement on behalf of the P.R.C. Up to that date, Pai Hsiang-kuo had been listed as foreign trade minister and Li as a vice minister. There had been no prior announcement of Li's promotion or of Pai's departure.

This method of announcing shifts of officials is usual in China. The significance of the switch is believed to be part of the continuing process of lessening the role of the army in national affairs, because, before he joined the Ministry of Foreign Trade in 1970, Pai had a distinguished career in the army. The new minister, Li Chiang, has been a vice minister of foreign trade since 1954, and his promotion is viewed as part of Chou's efforts to have responsible and technically competent civilians running China's ministries. He is expected to visit the U.S. in 1974 or 1975.

China has trade relations with more than 140 countries and trade agreements with 50 of them, according to the agency, and the importance of foreign trade to China's economy is obviously increasing.

The Canton Trade Fair

China had humored the sea-borne barbarians to the extent of tolerating foreign merchants at one port only, Canton. It was the tradesman's entrance, where they were treated as disreputable peddlers not permitted to cross the threshold into the house.

John Paton Davies, *Dragon by the Tail.*

Background. Canton, now called Kwangchow, for centuries was the center of Chinese overseas commerce carried by seagoing junks to such destinations as the Philippines, Java and Siam. Officially licensed merchant firms called "hongs" ran this commerce. The hongs faced a completely different situation when European traders appeared on the scene. The result was the banding together of the hongs into a "cohong" which was given monopoly over the trade. The cohong maintained tight control through large payments to local officials and to influential men in the emperor's court.

In the seventeenth century, the Canton trade was a Portuguese monopoly, as far as Europeans were concerned, until the British received permission to establish a factory there in 1684. By 1700 Spain, Holland, and France also were sharing the Canton trade, but the British share of the commerce was by far the largest.

The Manchu government placed Kwangtung province under a governor-general whose headquarters were at Canton. An imperial high commissioner was appointed to supervise all relations with foreigners and to prevent them from seeking formal diplomatic relations with Peking.

The Chinese made every effort to stop the unwanted foreigners from staying in China. Foreign women were prohibited from stepping on Chinese soil and traders were permitted to live only in the narrow confines of their factories. They were required to depart when the "trading season" ended—signaled by the shift of the monsoon winds to the southeast—returning to Hong Kong and Macao.[2]

Perhaps the chief cause of conflict between China and Great Britain was the opium trade. The Opium War of 1839 was triggered when China sought to stop the opium traffic as a moral and economic evil. Foreign powers won new concessions through imposed treaties after the Opium War. On 29 August 1842 the Chinese government capitulated and signed the first of a long series of unequal treaties that were to erode much of Chinese sovereignty. The 1842 Treaty of Nanking

---

[2] An absorbing fictional account of the period is found in James Clavell, *Tai-Pan* (New York: Atheneum, 1966). Another excellent book is Carl Crossman, *The China Trade* (Princeton, N.J.: The Pyne Press, 1972), which looks at the early days of the China market in terms of export paintings, furniture, silver, and other objects that were traded by China. A specialized book about an important aspect of early China trade is Yen-Ping Hao, *The Comprador in Nineteenth Century China* (Cambridge: Harvard University Press, 1970). A classic work is John King Fairbank, *Trade and Diplomacy on the China Coast: The Opening of the Treaty Ports, 1842-1854*, rev. ed. (Stanford: Stanford University Press, 1969).

designated Canton, Amoy, Foochow, Ningpo, and Shanghai as open to foreign trade; Canton continued to dominate trade with the outside world, and of the new treaty ports only Shanghai proved to be of great value.

Throughout its relations with China, which had begun with a trade treaty in 1844, the United States avoided seeking exclusive privileges, but insisted upon most-favored-nation treatment.

The Boer War had weakened British leverage in China at a crucial moment, so in 1899 London suggested that the United States should take the lead in convincing the great powers to maintain an open door for all nations' trade with China. The pronouncement of such a policy came that year in the form of a group of proposals issued by American Secretary of State John Hay to the interested powers, asking them (1) not to interfere with the treaty ports or preexisting foreign spheres of interest or leaseholds, (2) to agree that Chinese tariffs imposed should be collected equally on all merchandise of all nations, and (3) that there should be no discrimination among powers on matters of harbor dues or freight rates. The foreign acceptances of Hay's proposals were limited by some serious reservations, but he pronounced response to be favorable and declared that his Open Door policy had been accepted.

The foreign settlements in the treaty ports, given expanded privileges through the Open Door policy and the ensuing Chinese desire for more trade with the West, continued more or less in the same form—except for the interruption of the World War II occupation of Japan—until the Communist takeover of 1949, when all foreigners were expelled. At that time, Hong Kong and Macao, where it all started, saw their importance in the China trade enhanced once again.

Macao was "founded" by the Portuguese in 1557 to provide a base for the China trade. A rental was paid for the territory until the Portuguese declared it independent from China in 1849. This was not recognized by China until 1887, when Portugal undertook in return never to alienate Macao and its dependencies (outer islands Taipa and Coloane) without agreement with China. It was proclaimed an overseas province of Portugal in 1951. Since the signing of a secret treaty in 1967, it has been clear that Peking was calling the tune in Macao through its millionaire front man, Ho Yin.

Hong Kong was acquired by Britain from China in three stages: Hong Kong island (thirty-two square miles) by the Treaty of Nanking in 1842; Kowloon peninsula and Stonecutter's Island (3.75 square miles) by the First Convention of Peking in 1860; and the New Territories (365 square miles, consisting of a mainland area adjoining Kowloon and 235 adjacent islands) by a ninety-nine-year lease under the Second Convention of Peking in 1898. Most of the land area in Hong Kong is scheduled to revert to China in 1997, while Hong Kong island and Kowloon peninsula theoretically are ceded to Britain in perpetuity.

From the 1840s to the 1950s, apart from the Japanese occupation of 1942-45, Hong Kong served as a staging post and transshipment center for trade between China and the Western world. With the Korean War and the United Nations embargo on the shipment of strategic goods to China, much of this trade was cut off. Today, once again, Hong Kong is a major transshipment center for China, as well as a manufacturing and financial center in its own right.

It is interesting to note that in Canton, and later in Shanghai and other Chinese cities, foreigners were kept isolated. The troublesome intruders were given their own "quarter." This situation was perpetuated in the old "trading season" concept when foreigners could come back to Canton periodically from their homes in Hong Kong and Macao.

The Chinese preference for keeping foreigners at arm's length has not changed much since the early days of the China trade. Hong Kong has become, in a very real sense, the "foreign settlement" just outside China's doorstep rather than just inside, as was the case of the international settlement in Shanghai, for example.

The Modern Canton Trade Fair. The Canton Trade Fair convenes each year from 15 April to 15 May and from 15 October to 15 November. Emphasis at the fairs has been on Chinese exports but contracts for imports are also signed there. More and more of the bigger deals— such as for complete plants or jet aircraft—are now being signed in Peking or Shanghai. The future of the Canton fair as a trading institution seems secure, in fact it seems certain to be expanded.[3] Business

---

[3] For a thoughtful assessment of the Canton fair's relevance to Chinese foreign policy, see Daniel Tretiak, "The Canton Fair: An Academic Perspective," *China Quarterly*, no. 56 (October-December 1973), p. 740. Tretiak, who attended the fairs of 1972 and 1973, also provides an interesting sociological note; Chinese women play an important role in fair negotiations: "They seem to be more prominent, have higher status and more responsibility for decision-making than in other local institutions I have visited," said Tretiak, adding, "It is difficult to estimate what percentage of all Chinese negotiators are women, but a figure of 20 percent would not be surprising."

transacted at the fair sessions accounts for one-half of China's trade with developed nations and provides the most reliable gauge of China's current export and import capabilities and potential. The fair site recently shifted to larger facilities and 900 rooms were added to the adjacent Tung Feng Hotel.

Attendance at the Canton Trade Fair is by invitation only and these are usually extended by one of the foreign trading corporations or one of its agents. American businessmen just getting started in business with China should make their first contacts about the fair at:

> Division of PRC Affairs (556)
> Bureau of East-West Trade
> U.S. Department of Commerce
> Washington, D.C. 20230
> Tel: (202) 967-2908

It is sometimes possible to obtain an invitation to the fair by writing directly without previous contacts to:

> Chinese Export Commodities Fair
> Hai Chu Square
> Kwangchow, People's Republic of China

American firms were invited to attend the fair for the first time in the spring of 1972, and 38 American firms were represented, growing to 76 by the fall 1972 fair, and to 128 in the fall of 1973.[4]

The fall 1973 fair resulted in a turnover of "about $1.9 billion," but the big surprise was China's selling at what the Chinese described as "world market prices." Chinese economists were astonishingly accurate in their forecasting of world commodity prices.

American businessmen complained that Chinese fabrics shrank, that their standards on flammability were low, and that sometimes only small quantities of goods were available to them. There were also long delays in shipping and some forms of packaging were obsolete—600 dozen handkerchiefs packed loosely in a bale. There were also complaints about labeling—the Chinese refused to put American labels on their products. Although prices were somewhat higher than in 1972, Americans were generally satisfied on this score.[5]

---

[4] For a list of American firms represented at and individuals attending the fall 1973 Canton Trade Fair, see Appendix D.

[5] *China Report: Report of a Special Congressional Delegation,* July 1973; printed in *Congressional Record,* 7 November 1973.

The National Council for U.S.-China Trade

A result of President Nixon's visit to the P.R.C. was creation in the U.S. of the National Council for U.S.-China Trade. The joint communiqué issued in Shanghai at the conclusion of that visit said that both sides viewed bilateral trade as an area from which mutual benefits could be derived and agreed that trade was in the interests of the American and Chinese peoples. The two sides pledged themselves, to quote the communiqué, "to facilitate the progressive development of trade between their two countries."

Because the nations' economies are so different, it was inevitable that difficulties would develop. In China there is only one buyer and one seller—the state. The United States has an economy in which all 211 million citizens can be buyers and sellers, importers and exporters, if they so choose.

Mainly at Peking's request, it was decided during informal communication after President Nixon's visit that it would be desirable if a private organization could be set up in the U.S. to act as a trade go-between.

After consultation among the State Department, the Commerce Department, the Congress (Joint Economic Committee), and interested businessmen, the National Council on U.S.-China Trade was inaugurated in Washington in May 1973.

The National Council's main purpose is to act as a clearinghouse for information on China's trade, particularly with the U.S. Part of the urgency of China's request to set up such a body was the proliferation of a number of private "councils" and China trade organizations which promised American businessmen a key to Peking's trade doors. Much misinformation was conveyed and the Chinese became as confused as the State and Commerce departments were embarrassed at the antics of some of these "fast-buck" artists.

The National Council, which in October 1973 moved to permanent offices (Suite 513, 1100 17th St., N.W., Washington, D.C. 20036), will also provide publications (a monthly magazine began publication in January 1974) for both American businessmen and the appropriate trading organizations in the P.R.C.

Membership Categories. One criticism of the National Council throughout its first year of operation was that it seemed to be a "rich man's club." Membership is open to American corporations and is divided into two main categories: (1) corporations or business entities with sales or gross income of $50 million or more pay annual dues of $2,500, and (2) corporations with sales or gross income of less than $50 million pay annual dues of $1,000. The board of directors may grant exceptions to these membership requirements "where necessary or desirable to carry out the purpose of the National Council."

Because of these fees, which many smaller businessmen feel are exorbitant, there was a reaction and the earlier proliferation of "consultants" and China trade organizations made a comeback.

At the end of 1973, following a visit to Peking, the National Council's leaders decided to make some adjustments. One was the addition of a new membership category for firms doing less than $20 million in business each year, with the initial membership fee and annual dues tab of $500. Another added category is for importers and others doing under $10 million annual gross sales. They are now accorded an "affiliate" status which does not allow for a vote or for receiving other than import-related publications of the council. Affiliate members may also make use of the council's translation services at fees higher than regular members, but lower than would be available to nonmembers.

But it was still the intention of the Chinese, as well as the U.S. State and Commerce departments, to build an element of exclusiveness in the China trade, in terms of quality if not in size of companies, especially at the outset. Because the National Council will be instrumental in arranging trade exhibitions by American firms in China and by Chinese trading corporations in the United States—as well as playing the leading role in arranging exchanges of businessmen from the U.S. and trade officials from China and plant inspection tours—the National Council will be the focus of the U.S. side of trade with China for the near future.

Officers and Staff. The council's board of directors include the following: W. Michael Blumenthal, Bendix Corporation; Anthony J. A. Bryan, Cameron Iron Works; Donald C. Burnham, Westinghouse Electric Corp.; Edward W. Cook, Cook Industries, Inc.; Andrew E. Gibson, Interstate Oil Transport Co.; John W. Hanley, Monsanto Co.; William A. Hewitt, Deere & Co.; Donald W. Kendall, Pepsico; Joseph T. Kenneally, International Systems and Control Corp.; Robert H. Malott, FMC Corp.; David Packard, Hewlett-Packard Co.; Kurt S. Reinsburg, Associated Metals and Minerals Corp.; Charles W. Robinson, Marcona

Corp.; David Rockefeller, Chase Manhattan Bank; Fred M. Seed, Cargill, Inc.; Walter Sterling Surrey, Surrey, Karasik and Morse; Richard W. Wheeler, First National City Bank; Thornton A. Wilson, The Boeing Co.; Gabriel Hauge, Manufacturers Hanover Trust Co.

Officers are Burnham, chairman; Hewitt and Rockefeller, vice-chairmen; Phillips, president and executive director; Hauge, secretary-treasurer; and Surrey, counsel.

Phillips came to the post after five years as deputy representative of the U.S. to the United Nations, with the rank of ambassador (the Chinese explicitly requested that the operating head of the council have diplomatic rank). Phillips is from Massachusetts and was a state senator there from 1948 to 1953. He was subsequently appointed deputy assistant secretary of state for United Nations affairs and in 1958 became U.S. representative on the Economic and Social Council of the U.N. In 1960 Phillips was named Chase Manhattan Bank representative for the U.N. and manager of the bank's Canadian division. In 1965 he became president of the U.S. Council of the International Chamber of Commerce and secretary-treasurer of the U.S. Business and Industry Advisory Committee to the Organization for Economic Cooperation and Development (OECD). His father served as a second secretary in the U.S. legation in Peking in 1905.

The vice-president of the council is Eugene A. Theroux, a Washington attorney, who served as special counsel to the Joint Economic Committee of Congress, and visited China in 1972 and 1973. Nicholas Ludlow oversees publication of the monthly magazine and the compiling of handbooks on doing business with China. He was formerly an assistant Asian editor for *Business International* and has visited China. Lillian P. C. Leung, the council's chief translator and executive secretary, was born in Canton and grew up in Hong Kong before coming to the U.S. in 1969. She is fluent in Mandarin as well as in the Cantonese and Taiwanese dialects. Leung has a master of science degree in languages and linguistics.

The staff also includes writers and researchers who are assembling a library with resources ranging from *The China Letter* and *China Trade Report,* published in Hong Kong, to foreign trade monographs from U.S. and foreign universities, as well as Chinese publications.

The Chinese View of the Council. For the present at least, the National Council is the focal point in the United States as far as trade with China is concerned. P.R.C. officials regard the National Council as the counterpart of Peking's CPIT.

At the National Council's inaugural conference in May 1973, Minister Han Hsu, deputy chief of the liaison office of the P.R.C. in Washington, addressed the group. This was the first time an official of the P.R.C. had made an address in public in the United States (except for speeches at the United Nations). Han made it clear that Peking was counting heavily on the National Council.

Because Han's speech has never before been published and because it is an unusually frank (and extremely rare) statement by a P.R.C. official on Sino-American trade, we quote some pertinent excerpts:

> I am very happy to attend, on behalf of the Liaison Office of the People's Republic of China in the United States of America, the inaugural conference of the National Council for United States-China Trade. My colleagues and I would like to extend our sincere congratulations on the establishment of the National Council and to express our thanks to the Council for inviting us to attend this inaugural conference.
>
> Inspiring achievements have been attained in the relations between our two countries in the past year and more under the Principles of the Sino-U.S. Joint Communique published in Shanghai in February 1972. In particular, Sino-U.S. trade has developed rapidly. . . . The number of people from American industrial and commercial circles visiting the PRC is increasing daily.
>
> The National Council for United States-China Trade is founded precisely in accordance with the spirit of the principles of the Shanghai Communique. As everyone knows, there has existed the National Committee on United States-China Relations and the Committee of Scholarly Communication with the People's Republic of China which aim at promoting cultural, scientific and technological exchanges. Now there exists also the National Council for United States-China Trade which purpose is to promote trade relations between the two countries. This will not only help to further develop the trade relations between the two countries, but will also certainly be of benefit to the normalization of the relations between the two countries.
>
> One of the tasks of the Liaison Offices established in each other's capitals is to broaden the contacts in various fields between the two countries, including the expansion of trade relations between them. It can be anticipated that there will be quite a lot of contacts between the Council and our Liaison Office, and in your contacts with your counterpart—

the China Council for the Promotion of International Trade—
you can expect full cooperation and assistance from us.

May the work of the National Council for the United
States-China Trade be successful and fruitful.

While the speech may sound like an ordinary Chamber of Commerce effort, it is of great significance. Chinese Communist officials do not address American business groups without a specific purpose. The speech was a strong endorsement for steady progress in Sino-U.S. trade, and Han thus put Peking's stamp of approval on the National Council.

Some may feel that too much emphasis is placed on the role of the National Council, but in the absence of diplomatic relations between the two countries, it is the principal U.S. focal point for trade. In the longer run, formal mutual diplomatic recognition by the United States and China could shift the National Council's chores to the more usual channels of the Commerce Department, State Department, Export-Import Bank, and commercial banks.

Trade Imbalance in U.S. Favor. Sino-American trade in 1973 showed a balance in the U.S.'s favor of about 16 to 1. Although Peking's stated policy is balanced trade with each partner, the tolerance of the imbalance shows the Chinese are willing to pay a price—at least temporarily—to get trade with the U.S. on a solid footing.

President Phillips of the National Council for U.S.-China Trade emphasized, however, in a September 1973 speech that such an imbalance cannot go on forever.[6] Quoting Chairman Mao, who has said that "the Chinese people wish to resume and expand international trade," Phillips called attention to "a Chinese principle that American firms would ignore at their peril. It is that trade must be conducted on the basis of equality and mutual benefit." He added that a problem was already developing in this regard, since "of a total Sino-U.S. trade this year [1973] of some $800-$900 million, only some $50 million is expected by way of imports from China."

Phillips has assured American importers that the council will be working closely with them to overcome difficulties which they may encounter in buying from China. Phillips stressed that "this is not solely a Chinese job. The United States Congress, in my opinion, must act

---

[6] Speech before the International Management and Development Institute, New York, 26 September 1973.

favorably and promptly on legislation permitting the extension of most-favored-nation tariff treatment to China."

Most-Favored-Nation Status. Although MFN status is not the only roadblock to increased U.S.-China trade (among others: blocked assets in each country, lack of standardization and quality control in Chinese packaging and labeling, lack of market information on both sides), it is a significant hurdle, and it is viewed by the Nixon administration as slowing progress in China trade. Although the National Council is supposed to be a private organization, it takes its policy cues from the White House. Excerpts from a letter of 18 September 1973 from Phillips to the acting chairman of the House Ways and Means Committee sum up the administration's views at the time:

> The National Council for U.S.-China Trade is a private non-profit association of American firms, both large and small, interested in importing from and exporting to the People's Republic of China. In the course of our activities, we have determined that the failure of the Committee on Ways and Means to provide for the possibility of extension of most-favored-nation treatment to the People's Republic of China would have several undesirable effects. Among the factors to be considered are the following:
>
> —American importers are severely handicapped with respect to developing trade with China as long as Chinese goods are subject to Column 2 duties.
>
> —American exporters, many of whom hope to make sales of very expensive technology and goods to China, recognize that, without foreign exchange earned from exports, China will be unable to make substantial American purchases.
>
> —China, as you know, seeks to balance her trade bilaterally wherever possible. At present, there is a very strong and growing imbalance of trade between the U.S. and China. It seems likely that the value of our exports would exceed imports from China by a ratio of 15 to 1 this year.
>
> —The Joint Communique issued at Shanghai at the conclusion of President Nixon's visit pledged our country to work to facilitate the development of trade with China. Maintenance of trade legislation which prevents liberalized tariff treatment for Chinese goods would appear to be contrary to the spirit of the Shanghai communique.
>
> We recognize that the current controversy surrounding Title V of H.R. 6767 relates not to China but to certain policies of the Soviet Union. We appreciate the concerns of members of the House over these Soviet policies and practices,

but we wish to point out that to deny the possibility of trade benefits to the Soviet Union would have the effect of very seriously jeopardizing those same benefits for China.

The issue, indeed, transcends bilateral trade. The Chinese would appear to be justifiably disappointed should our policy towards the Soviet Union on trade have a significant and damaging, if unintended effect on our trade policy with China.

Our recommendation, therefore, is that Title V of the pending "Trade Reform Act of 1973" be retained as proposed.

Should the committee decide to delete Title V for reasons related to policies of the Soviet Union and Central Europe, we urge prompt and favorable consideration of a separate bill which would permit the President to conclude a trade agreement, embracing most-favored-nation tariff treatment, with the People's Republic of China.

By November 1973, however, when the National Council's first delegation visited China to attend the Canton Trade Fair, Chinese officials made known their disappointment that the MFN issue was linked to Soviet policy on Jewish emigration.

As if to make certain that China was never accused of preventing emigration, the Chinese allowed increasing numbers of persons of all ages to leave for Hong Kong during 1973. Under a tacit understanding with the Chinese, Hong Kong had expected no more than 50 arrivals per day, but in 1971—after a lull since the Cultural Revolution—the figure had picked up and exceeded the annual "quota" (of approximately 17,500) and had reached 21,000. During 1973 the rate of arrivals in Hong Kong was running at well over twice the 1972 figure of 26,000 going into November. The Chinese government imposes no tax or other penalties on emigrants once approval is given.

The nudging by the National Council and others seemed to have some effect. On 12 December 1973 a special congressional delegation, which visited China in August 1973, proposed that the United States end trade discrimination against China and grant MFN status.

Headed by Senator Warren G. Magnuson (D-Wash.), the eight-member delegation stated in its report that the Chinese were concerned about their trade deficit with the United States.[7]

"We could not deny that unless the present ratio in our trade with China is redressed to some extent, the level of trade, not to mention growth, could not be sustained," the report said. It added that the dele-

---

[7] *China Report: Report of a Special Congressional Delegation.*

gation also told the Chinese that China must produce goods which meet U.S. consumer demands, even to the extent of gearing some of their industries specifically to U.S. needs.

The delegation recommended that Congress should as soon as possible authorize President Nixon to negotiate MFN status for China. This would mean giving China trade treatment—in level of tariffs and in other areas—equal to that extended to Western countries and Poland and Yugoslavia.

The delegation also suggested a study of financing trade, including the possible creation of a Sino-American Bank similar to the U.S. Export-Import Bank. In April 1974, Senate Democratic leader Mike Mansfield said he would shortly introduce legislation to grant China MFN trade status.

In addition, Christopher Phillips called for repeal of the current prohibition of entry into the United States of certain furs—such as ermine, mink and fox—produced in the P.R.C. He cited this as an "unwarranted irritant in our relations with China," pointing out that domestic producers will have the benefit of protective decrees in the pending bill against "injurious competition."

Chinese Trade Exhibition Planned. On returning from his November 1973 mission to China, Phillips announced that China would send its first commercial mission to the United States early in 1974 and follow up with a trade exhibition, probably in 1975.[8] Phillips said it was also agreed that the United States would hold a trade exhibition in China.

Details of the exhibitions, he said, would be worked out when the Chinese mission visited the United States. But he thought the Chinese would probably be eager to have their exhibition in the United States before any American exhibition in China because of the imbalance in the burgeoning trade between the two countries.

Phillips and his hosts, the CPIT, also agreed on regular visits so that each side could have a clearer idea of each other's needs and expectations.

Gabriel Hauge, chairman of the board of the Manufacturers Hanover Trust Company, talked with officials of the Bank of China about the role American banks might play in promoting trade expansion. The Chinese have always said they would not accept foreign credits, but in 1973 Peking agreed to a number of "deferred payment" plans—as they

---

[8] Press release, National Council for U.S.-China Trade, 20 November 1973.

44

prefer to call them—in which interest payments are downplayed but very much a part of the agreements.

At present, agricultural commodities account for a large part of American exports to China, but Phillips said the National Council delegation gained the impression that the strongest interest of the Chinese was in the areas of "high technology." He cited the development of China's offshore oil reserves: The Chinese were firm and clear in saying that they were not interested in any forms of joint ventures in the development of their natural resources. "But experience indicates," he said, "that ways will be found, in their own interest, to exploit their petroleum reserves."

Official Views on Trade. Henry Kissinger's sixth trip to China, in November 1973, illustrated the positive way in which Sino-American relations were developing. The wording of the communiqué at the end of the visit—language suggested by China—made the Taiwan issue seem less urgent.

In addition to calling for "a number of new exchanges for the coming year [1974]," the communiqué said specifically of trade: "Trade between the two countries has developed rapidly during the past year. The two sides held that it is in the interest of both countries to take measures to create conditions for further development of trade on the basis of equality and mutual benefit."

Kissinger's three-and-a-half days of talks with Chou, and a long meeting with Mao, showed Peking's interest in the relationship in general and trade in particular.

Three years ago, few would have expected that the Peking-Washington relationship would have progressed so far, so fast. Three years from now, the relationship could progress further "on the basis of equality and mutual benefit," much further than even today's boldest assumptions foresee.

5

China as an Exporter and Importer

A line repeated often by Chinese officials whom the authors met in Peking and other cities is: "We are an underdeveloped country, we have much to do." The evidence indicates that the idea of catching up with the rest of the world, in an industrial sense, bears heavily on Chinese thinking and planning. Chinese officials have been studying the Japanese economy for several years, noting those techniques that may be applicable in the Chinese situation. Similar studies, though on a less comprehensive basis, are underway already in the United States (with the cooperation of the National Council for U.S.-China Trade) and Western Europe.

Another way of describing China's penchant for catching up with the industrialized world is that Peking wants to acquire an industrial and technological revolution of its own. In some respects, the thinking parallels that of the Great Leap Forward period when the realization struck home that China needed a rapid surge forward. But the backyard steel furnaces, symbols of the Great Leap, were too crude and the net result was failure.

Shrewd Trading and Foreign Credits

The upcoming "Great Leap" or "instant industrial revolution" will depend on heavy borrowings of technology and, we believe, capital from Japan and the West. In other words, accelerated foreign trade and use of foreign expertise and long-term credits—controlled and spread around among a number of sources in order to avoid dependency on any one source—will be China's means of paying for its instant industrial revolution.

Officials in Peking will bridle at the use of the word "instant" since they abhor any suggestion that crash programs are under way to correct the nation's gaps in industry and technology. But beyond the basic priority goal of solving the people-food equation, China wants to industrialize as soon as possible. Shrewdness in foreign trade, which will allow hard currency earnings as needed, and a gradual acceptance of long-term credits appear to be the methods which the Chinese will use.

The Chinese have been specific in telling some Americans at the Canton fair how they will do it. They say they can do it, first, by such trading transactions as their recent purchases of wheat and their simultaneous sales of rice, in which they take advantage of the world market price differentials to profit substantially. They have, for example, generated enough hard currency in international trade recently to enable them to purchase ten Boeing 707s at a cost of about $125 million. Their purchases of two RCA satellite ground stations for communications were substantially in cash. Recent large grain and related purchases by China have involved large sums of cash and relatively short-term payouts.

Shrewd trading will not be sufficient, however, to generate enough funds to pay for the massive purchases of sophisticated machinery and equipment for the technological revolution.

That leaves acceptance of long-term credits or some similar form of developmental financing as the only road for Peking to follow. There is no question about the international—especially American—financial community's willingness to provide such developmental credits.

To develop the full capacity of its mineral resources China will require a heavy investment in technology and equipment. Substantial lead time is required to accomplish this, so five- and ten-year credits will not be sufficient. Peking has the bargaining power—not to mention the enthusiasm on the part of Western and Japanese banks—to acquire long-term credit, and China's reputation for business integrity and adherence to financial obligations is very good.

Our contention is that China is so vast, her potential for development so immense, that extensive borrowings can be undertaken without sacrificing sovereignty or becoming overly dependent on any one country. Chinese have for years been studying British finance and banking operations, and we can foresee the not-so-distant day when teams of young Peking bankers visit banks in the U.S. to learn modern banking techniques, just as Chinese aircraft technicians have come to Seattle to study the Boeing 707 jet aircraft.

The fact is that, while Peking continues to profess policies of self-reliance and disinclination to accept credits of any kind, it is already doing so. The long-term lines of credit accepted so far are thinly disguised as "foreign aid" or "deferred payments." For example, Peking has negotiated deferred payments for $800 million of the $1.2 billion worth of complete plants ordered in 1973. Usual terms are one-quarter down with further payments commencing after a three-year moratorium and continuing for five years. Officially, no interest is charged, but suppliers calculate interest in setting their prices. For the first time since its disastrous experience with Soviet loans and tech-nicians in the 1950s, China has contracted foreign loans—in effect, if not in official or admitted form.

China is also borrowing on the Eurodollar market in London. The Chinese have come to the conclusion that not even they can be entirely self-sufficient. Their alternatives are to borrow discriminately or fail to develop and modernize economically. China has already begun to accept limited credits, but has not come out of the closet and admitted this as policy. Such policy statements, we believe, will come in time.

Five-Year Plan Suggests Specific Markets

One of the best indicators of China's trade potential by specific markets is the nation's current Five-Year Plan (1971-75). Although available details of the plan are sketchy, comments on the plan by Chinese officials help fill in some of the gaps. The main priority of the plan is agricultural plants and equipment. The plan stresses the use of tractors for building a mechanized agricultural capacity (including some imports of tractors, combines, and other equipment) in a short period of time. The next priority is given mining equipment for development of the nation's mineral resources. Also given high priority in the plan are the petroleum, chemicals, and construction sectors. Requirements in these sectors are influencing the Chinese pattern of imports.

Domestic manufacturing of machine tools, oxygen generators, air compressors and all kinds of motors and pumps is being emphasized, but until self-sufficiency can be achieved in their production, some imports will continue. The same is true of trucks and various other kinds of motor vehicles. China's highest priority for imports in the industrial

49

sector will, however, be in sophisticated fields such as aircraft, communications equipment, and perhaps computer technology.

The importance to the P.R.C. of a well-developed communications system for internal security and the operation of the economy is obvious. The military establishment places enormous demands on Chinese communications manufacturers for specialized military equipment.

The program for the dispersal of industry away from the coast requires the integration of the communications system and its expansion into previously underdeveloped areas. The P.R.C. has some interest in increasing the production of microwave and television broadcasting equipment and initiating the production of high-capacity multiplexing equipment. However, the use of wired loudspeakers still remains the basic means for transmitting announcements or propaganda to the people. Thus, during the current Five-Year Plan there is the requirement to increase significantly the output and raise the technical level of communications equipment to satisfy the demands of both the economy and the military establishment.

But China still is unable to produce highly advanced telecommunications apparatus in large quantities. Therefore, the importation of such equipment from the West continues on a priority basis. American manufacturers are being asked to supply some of this equipment, but they are facing competition from Western Europe and Japan.

American experts believe that during the current Five-Year Plan China will show progress in the production of solid state instrumentation and at the same time achieve the capability to mass produce sophisticated instruments which at present are handmade. But the need for advanced instrumentation such as integrated circuit testers, computer test equipment, and microwave test equipment will grow with the continued development of China's electronics industry.

When China achieves an increased production of instruments, it can be expected to offer more of them for export. By 1975, China could have the capability to export, at very competitive prices, large quantities of simple transistorized test equipment.

Peking planners remark privately that they believe computers will help speed the technological and industrial revolution. It is believed that the bulk of China's computer inventory (including imported computers) is used by the military. Imported and domestic computers are being used in China's nuclear and missile programs for weapons design, vibration studies, and trajectory analysis. The Chinese have stated that they have used their DMJ-3 analog model in solving problems related to atomic weapons, guided missiles and aircraft location (probably air traffic control).[1] They also have said that the DMJ-16B analog computer has been used for electrical network analysis and that the DJS-7 digital computer is suitable for process control. They have used unspecified models for processing census data and very likely are using both imported and domestically produced models in accounting operations, for inventory control, and in economic planning.

It is an aim of the current Five-Year Plan to increase production of computers in response to rising requirements. Despite the expected advances, however, Chinese production of computers during the next few years will not satisfy, either quantitatively or qualitatively, domestic requirements. Moreover, in view of the fast pace of computer developments in the West, China's technological lag in computers may increase even further. Therefore, the Chinese will continue to require substantial imports, and therefore sophisticated computer equipment and specialized software comprise a very substantial potential market for U.S. manufacturers during the next decade. Advanced copy machines and assorted business machines should find a market in China also.

Chinese Exports

Up-to-date lists of Chinese exports may be obtained from the U.S. Department of Commerce. The department's 1973 list is as follows:

Live animals
Meat and meat preparations
Fish and fish preparations
Rice
Fruit and vegetables
Tea
Hides and skins, undressed
Soybeans
Tung oil
Silk, silk yarn, fabrics, and manufactures
Tungsten ore and concentrates
Glass, glassware, and pottery
Hog bristles

---

[1] *Ta Kung Pao*, Hong Kong, 1 May 1969, p. 1.

Machinery and equipment used in perfumery, pharmacy, and
    insecticide manufacture
Coal, coke, and briquettes
Crude petroleum
Bicycles
Furs, dressed (except seven embargoed furs)
Handicrafts and arts
Musical instruments
Clothing
Tin

The commodity distribution of Chinese exports has not changed as sharply as the import pattern over the past decade. Raw and processed agricultural products make up about three-quarters of the total, with a slowly growing share for such processed goods as cotton and silk textiles, canned fruits and vegetables, meat, and soybean products. The big change has been the increase in textile exports from about 5 percent to nearly 25 percent of total exports. Mineral sales abroad, both ores and metals, have declined sharply because of increased domestic use.

Other manufactured goods exported are mainly glassware and crockery, aluminum and enamelware pots and pans, thermos jugs, flashlights and batteries, kerosene lanterns, hardware, and building materials. More recent exports include bicycles, electric fans, small garden tractors, radios and cameras, and some simple machinery. Also important as foreign exchange earners are traditional handicraft items such as rattanware, brocade, carved wood and stone, jade and ivory, lacquerware, porcelain, and ornamental brass. Export progress during the 1970s will depend on the performance of the agricultural sector, success in industrialization at home, and the lowering of trade barriers abroad.

Chinese Imports

The following is a list of commodities which the Chinese are currently importing or appear likely to import in the near future:

Wheat
Corn
Cotton
Sugar
Jute

Synthetic yarns and fibers
Nitrogenous fertilizers
Urea
Organic chemicals and dyestuffs
Rubber and rubber products
Plastic materials
Industrial diamonds
Metalworking equipment, including transfer machines, and
    numerically controlled machine tools
Pulp and papermaking equipment
Ball, needle, and roller bearings
Gas turbine peaking units
Computers and calculating machines
Telecommunications equipment
Scientific instrumentation
Nuclear power station equipment
Complete plants and technology for steelmaking and finishing;
    petrochemicals; synthetic fibers; ammonia, urea, and
    other nitrogenous fertilizers; phosphate fertilizers;
    television tubes; and petroleum refineries
Pumps, centrifuges and filtering equipment
Mining and construction machinery
Agricultural machinery
Commercial jet-transport aircraft
Airport ground support equipment, including aircraft
    landing systems
Trucks
Diesel locomotives and other railway rolling stock
Paper and paperboard equipment
Iron and steel scrap
Steel structurals, plates and sheets
Steel tube and pipe, seamless
Aluminum and semimanufactures
Copper and semimanufactures
Nickel and semimanufactures
Petroleum exploration, drilling and production equipment
High-pressure compressors
Offshore drilling equipment
Power generation equipment [2]

---

[2] For the commodities actually being traded between the U.S. and China, see
complete trade composition figures for 1972 and 1973 in Appendix A.

To summarize, China's major import categories are machinery and vehicles, steel and nonferrous metals, chemicals and dyes, natural rubber, textile fibers, wheat, sugar and manufactured fertilizer. Nitrogen fertilizer may be considered an alternative to more grain imports as each ton of chemical fertilizer should boost food production by about two tons.

Some important changes in the import pattern have taken place over the past decade. Greatly increased imports of food grains and fertilizer reflect steady population growth and rapid urbanization. Meanwhile China has found it possible to reduce imports of cotton and sugar due to increased home production. Petroleum imports, which amounted to over $100 million annually at the beginning of the 1960s, have been completely eliminated.

Imports of grain are expected to continue to be brisk. The U.S. Department of Agriculture said China is expected to import a record $1 billion worth of agricultural products from the United States during 1973-74. Late grain harvests in 1973 may have been as good as the bumper crops reported in August, but demand would still result in imports four to five times greater than the 1972 total, valued at $200 million.[3]

During the 1973-74 fiscal year, China is expected to import about 9 million tons of grain, including 6.5 million tons of wheat. Of that figure, almost 4 million is expected to come from the United States and the rest from Canada and Australia. The Chinese also are expected to buy from 2.5 million to 3 million tons of seed grains, including corn, from the U.S. during 1974.

---

[3] U.S. Department of Agriculture, *Foreign Agriculture*, December 1973, p. 3.

6
Toward the Year 2000

China Reenters the World

The last thirty years of the nineteenth century were marked in China by national humiliation. The country was exploited by foreign powers who battled one another for choice concessions. China was weakened by the loss of territories and its internal structure crumbled.

The corresponding years in this century may be regarded by historians as the time when China reentered the world, taking a second chance at associating with the Western world, this time on more equal terms. The first seventy years of the twentieth century were incredibly eventful for China: the Boxer Rebellion of 1900; the founding of the Chinese Republic by Sun Yat-sen in 1912; the establishment and growth of the Chinese Communist Party; the prolonged civil war between Nationalists and Communists and China's war against Japan; the founding of the People's Republic of China in 1949; the removal to Taiwan of the Nationalist government; the organization of Chinese society by the Communist regime; the Korean War; the boom years of Chinese societies in Hong Kong, Taiwan, and Singapore; the P.R.C. development of nuclear capability; and finally, U.S.-China rapprochement.

In the quarter-century that lies ahead until the year 2000, there is the bright possibility of a China characterized by even more stability and self-respect. On the dark side, there is a nagging danger of war along the Sino-Soviet border. It was that persistent Soviet threat, as we have seen, that probably nudged China into a more rapid reentry into the international society, especially into ties with the U.S., than some of its leaders might have desired.

Let us turn back briefly to the crucial last thirty years of the nineteenth century. Political and economic exploitation by Westerners during the period was accompanied by Western cultural inroads. Christianity, which enjoyed the protection of extraterritoriality, saw its positive contributions diluted by resentment which resulted in sporadic violence, although the missionary work in medicine and education had considerable influence on Chinese intellectuals.

Chinese officialdom of the period, however, could not cope with the ideas imported from the West. They recognized the superiority of Western arms and industry but failed to understand the civilization which produced such technology. For this reason and for more complex reasons found in the intricacies of Chinese thinking, tradition and culture, the leadership was unwilling to make basic changes in institutions necessary to adapt to the West or to borrow techniques selectively from the West as Japan had done.

In many ways the shoe is on the other foot today. It is China, not the West, that is dictating the terms of entry to the China market, and, of course, that is how it should be. The recollections of past injustices and humiliation at the hands of foreigners—usually thought of as confined to the Opium War and Boxer periods, but actually including the Soviet experience—have cemented a spirit of self-reliance in the Chinese attitude. This includes a thoroughness on the part of Chinese officials based in the U.S. trying to learn about a society which is different and perplexing to them. The exchange of students can only be beneficial. The day may not be far off when Shanghai and Peking university students are seen on campus at Harvard, Yale, Stanford, or Hawaii's East-West Center.

The point is that China has changed its approach to the West. By the end of this century, Sino-American friendship could progress to a breadth that is as unimaginable today as was the prospect of an American president visiting Peking only a few years ago. Now it is time for the West, particularly the United States, to complete its change of attitude toward China, begun by the Nixon-Kissinger visits.

In the area of trade, American businessmen will have the fascinating opportunity to participate in the building of a new commercial and technological relationship between the world's most populous society and the world's most highly industrialized society.

Among the opportunities and challenges for American traders—from oil executives to importers of chopsticks—is the chance to get to know China and the Chinese in the context of today and the future, rather than regarding that country in terms of the cliches of the past. As for the prospects for trade itself, the best available opinion on the question is that the development of Sino-American trade will increase much more rapidly than was believed possible or probable only a few years ago.

Expert Opinion on the Future of Trade

In attempting to forecast the future of Sino-American trade the authors solicited opinions from prominent Americans in the field. In late 1973 each was requested to give an opinion on the level of future U.S.-China trade, looking as far ahead as each thought reasonable. As the reader will see, there is a strong feeling of optimism for the long-term future of the China market.

Louis J. Mulkern, senior vice-president of the Bank of America in San Francisco, estimates that two-way trade between the United States and China will range between $1.5 and $1.8 billion by 1975. He noted that U.S.-China trade in 1973 constituted about one-quarter of China's total trade and "at this point it seems unlikely that China will allow it to exceed this level." If China's total trade doubles by 1980 to about $10 billion, the U.S. portion would be about $2.5 billion. Oil exploration offers the possibility of increased U.S. exports to China. Several U.S. companies are already exploring these possibilities, Mulkern said, and "are likely to find the Chinese interested in oil rigs and peripheral equipment as well as petrochemical industry supplies." While many economists cling to the notion that China will shun long-term credits, Mulkern sees Chinese borrowing as a definite possibility for the future:

> it appears that China's need to modernize her economy dictates sizable overseas borrowings. Infrastructure, power generation, exploitation of natural resources, industrial development will all necessitate China's tapping the surplus savings of the West and Japan. More than trade, this appears to be the intriguing potential for the West's relationships with China over the coming years.

Fred C. Hung, professor of economics at the University of Hawaii, believes that even with the most favorable economic and political conditions, U.S. trade with China by 1980 will form only slightly more than 1 percent of the United States's total foreign trade. This estimate was based on the following figures: China's total foreign trade in 1970 was estimated at $4.3 billion, or about 6 percent of China's GNP; the U.S. trade figure for 1970 was $82 billion, about 8 percent of the GNP. If both countries double their GNP and foreign trade in the ten years between 1970 and 1980 (representing a 7 or 8 percent annual growth, which Hung termed "the upper limit" of optimism), and if the U.S. can capture 20 percent of China's foreign trade (again, "the upper limit"), then the value of Sino-American trade will be $2 billion, or about 1.3 percent of the $160 billion projected total U.S. foreign trade. Professor Hung is very doubtful that the U.S. can ever capture anything like 20 percent of China's foreign trade.

David C. Buxbaum, the Mandarin-speaking president of May Lee Industries, Inc., in New York, has been very outspoken in contradicting pessimistic estimates of Sino-American trade. He feels that China has clearly shown by its actions a willingness to facilitate trade with the United States and that the recent establishment of the China National Technical Import Corporation is another move by China signalling its desire to once again import whole plants and technology on a substantial basis.

Referring to an article which he wrote recently on the subject, Buxbaum noted that China has evolved considerably from traditional times, although certain modern institutions and geographical locations of foreign trade are similar to traditional practices. In the article he said:

> China has shown her desire to trade with the United States and has exhibited care, precision and sophistication in drawing up her contracts and in performing her international obligations. China is both a desirable and reliable trading partner and hopefully will be accorded most-favored-nation status so that Chinese goods may be purchased more inexpensively by the American consumer, and so that China can more readily purchase American goods with the foreign exchange she thus earns. The traditional friendship between the peoples of China and the American people should, and someday shall, be permitted to blossom more fully as the tempo of cultural, political and economic exchanges increases. Chinese-American trade has and should continue to develop with rapidity.[1]

[1] David C. Buxbaum, "American Trade with the People's Republic of China: Some Preliminary Perspectives," *Columbia Journal of Transnational Law*, vol. 12, no. 1 (1973).

William W. Whitson, director of China studies at the RAND Corporation and editor of a recently published book on trading with China,[2] believes that political considerations will determine trade levels. He stated:

> My own view is that the boundaries of China trade within the next fifteen years may be significantly influenced by the outcome of succession in China. It seems clear that Chou En-lai and his group of pragmatists are committed to a substantial import of foreign technology, partly in order to mollify the demands of a potentially consumer-oriented, increasingly restive younger generation, but also to prove to older leaders of the radical left that Chouist detente with the industrial west makes sense. Accordingly, under a Chouist regime, Sino-American trade might expand to several billion dollars by 1990.

Dr. Harned Pettus Hoose is an attorney involved in international business and a consulting professor of international business at the Graduate School of Business Administration, University of Southern California. He was born and raised in China, lived there for twenty years, and speaks fluent Chinese. He has made several recent trips to China.

Hoose is very optimistic on the prospects of trade between the United States and China. He says the Chinese will pay for the massive purchases of sophisticated machinery and equipment for the industrial revolution by using its vast mineral and petroleum resources to earn hard currency. He estimates that China has the third largest petroleum resources in the world. Hoose claims that P.R.C. officials have mentioned $5 billion as a likely level which Sino-American two-way trade could reach within five to eight years.

Arthur C. Miller, the editor of the leading American-owned publication on U.S.-China trade, *The China Letter* of Hong Kong, stated that in talks with China's trading officials he got the impression that China is prepared to accept a large trade imbalance with the United States as long as U.S. purchases from China continue to expand at a steady pace. Eventual granting of most-favored-nation treatment for U.S. imports of goods from China will be a tremendous boon to Sino-U.S. trade. He estimated that Sino-U.S. trade through the rest of the 1970s and assuredly beyond that will total at least $1 billion a year.

---

[2] William W. Whitson, *Doing Business with China: American Trade Opportunities in the 1970s* (New York: Praeger Publishers, Inc., 1974).

59

Miller said it would not surprise him at all if U.S.-China trade reached the $3 to $4 billion level by 1980.

Professor Robert F. Dernberger, associate chairman, Department of Economics, University of Michigan, felt that the estimates he made in 1970 are still valid when allowance is made for inflation and for the fact that most of the recent jump in U.S. exports to China is accounted for by the Chinese need to import agricultural commodities.[3] He estimated that in 1980 U.S. exports will amount to $650 million and imports $250 million.

Charles E. Young, vice-president of the First National City Bank, stated that rather than try to estimate future trade figures, it would be more rational to discuss a factor of crucial importance for Sino-U.S. trade. There is a large trade imbalance and it is doubtful that China can afford to allow this deficit to continue for any length of time. Hence continued improvement in trade will depend on the extension of trade credits to China. At the same time China's acceptance of such financing, assuming it is forthcoming in the first place, will probably hinge on an assurance that its exports will find larger markets in the U.S. This assurance, in turn, will depend on the legal resolution of blocked Chinese funds in the U.S. and the easing of tariff questions.

William W. Clarke, director, Division of P.R.C. Affairs, Bureau of East-West Trade, U.S. Department of Commerce, was similarly wary of making long-range quantitative forecasts. He said predictions beyond a year or two amounted to "guesswork." He said that he was confident the blocked assets question would be solved soon, "hopefully by the middle of 1974." Technically, he said, without a resolution of this problem, Chinese ships entering San Francisco harbor, for example, could be legally attached by American claimants against China.

Clarke acknowledged that U.S. government forecasting of U.S.-China trade figures had varied widely in recent years. "We are, however, fairly certain what the levels will be for calendar 1974. We see American exports rising to about $1.15 billion. China's sales to the United States, we calculate, will be about $100 million."

Kenneth E. Arndt, a vice-president of the Chase Manhattan Bank, meets regularly with P.R.C. officials in Washington as part of Chase's new correspondent banking relationship with the Bank of China. He

---

[3] Robert F. Dernberger, "Prospects for Trade Between China and the United States," in *China Trade Prospects and United States Policy,* ed. Alexander Eckstein (New York: National Committee on U.S.-China Relations, 1970).

said, "the real opportunity for greatly increased trade comes with the possibility of credit," and warned that "there are definite limits to the development that China can finance itself."

Arndt said unless the blocked account problem, certain immigration laws, and an outstanding $22.5 million U.S. Export-Import Bank claim are overcome soon, "it is possible we will lose out on some potentially attractive trade activity." He concluded that "in estimating future U.S. trade with the P.R.C., past developments in the political sphere teach us to be cautious. A continued upward growth cannot be taken for granted."

Alexander Eckstein, professor of economics, Center for Chinese Studies, University of Michigan, and a member of the board of directors of the National Committee on U.S.-China Relations, notes the "clear indications" that the Chinese are investing heavily in a number of high technology projects.

In predicting the level of U.S.-China trade for 1980, Dr. Eckstein quoted from a paper which he had just prepared:

> In contrast to the past pattern, we would expect China's imports to rise somewhat faster than its exports, essentially for two kinds of interrelated reasons. The Chinese will have at their disposal some medium term credits which will enable them to maintain a trade deficit. Moreover, assuming such credits will grow in volume, China will have less need of a trade surplus than when it was repaying Soviet credits between 1955 and 1965.
>
> It is improbable that over the long run the U.S. will supply more than 29 percent of PRC imports or that Japan and the U.S. combined will provide more than 50 percent.
>
> This means that U.S. exports to China would be projected at about $1.5 billion in 1980, more than twice the current level.[4]

Finally, some recent remarks of Charles Freeman, the State Department P.R.C. political desk officer, are worth considering. In early June 1974 he said, "By 1980, U.S.-China trade will total $4 billion to $5 billion. . . . Progress toward full diplomatic relations will follow the trade expansion, but more slowly."

---

[4] Alexander Eckstein and Bruce Reynolds, "Sino-American Trade Prospects and Policy" (Paper delivered at panel on *Trends, Prospects and Policies for East-West Trade*, meetings of American Economic Association and the Association for Comparative Economic Studies, New York (29 December 1973).

Freeman confirmed that Peking has told Washington that expansion of trade, as well as development of wider relations, will grow step by step. And he added, "Things are slow now because China wishes periods of pause in advancing toward full relations, and we are now in one such period of pause. I don't expect we will break very much new ground in the immediate future."

Freeman pointed out that this is because Peking wants the United States first to break diplomatic relations with Taiwan. As part of the 1972 understanding with Peking, the number of U.S. troops on Taiwan was cut from 9,000 to fewer than 5,000, "and they will go down again dramatically this year," Freeman said. "We are removing them with the prospect in mind of improving our relations."

7
Conclusion

The average worker living in a Peking suburb today earns about sixty yuan each month, or roughly thirty dollars. His living expenses are correspondingly low. Housing and utilities cost about ten yuan, food bills run about twenty yuan, a pair of trousers costs twenty yuan, and purchase would depend on whether or not he had any of his cloth ration quota left. To buy a bicycle—there are nearly two million bicycles in Peking—the average worker would need to save almost three months' pay, or about 150 yuan.

By the year 2000, the average worker in a Peking suburb should be earning much more. Although there will be more than one billion Chinese in the P.R.C. by then, many of the goals of the government will have been realized. The basic requirements for achievement of the goals will be, as we have discussed, continuation of a period of relative domestic political stability, satisfactory handling of the people-food equation, and a world power context free from devastating wars. There must be continuing cooperation, to some degree, among the major powers; the balance of power must continue.

By 1980, and coming into full flower by the year 2000, the impact of China's economic potential will be felt around the world. In the opinion of the authors, the progress that can be made by China—the potential for domestic development, including limited participation by foreigners—is tremendous.

The benefits to the rest of the world from relating to China and to trading and dealing financially with China will also be significant. For Americans, there are greater prospects for trade than any political or economic experts have prophesized in the past, although this will depend on the degree to which the Chinese will accept foreign credits.

There are aspects of the new China which are very difficult for most Americans to understand, let alone view with sympathy. The kind of group effort on which Peking is relying for progress is very different from Western society's emphasis on the individual. China has the chance, should its "millions of successors" so choose, or have chosen for them by their leaders, to steer a path somewhere between what Australian author Ross Terrill has called the "jungle of capitalism and the prison of communism." [1]

What about the dynamism of Mao's revolution? There is always the tendency for any organization to become so institutionalized and professional that vitality is lost. This could happen to the party, army, and government of China as it has to others in history, and the revolutionary zeal would be dissipated.[2]

In the youthful United States of America, Thomas Jefferson said he would favor a new revolution every twenty years to head off this drift to malaise. There are signs that this problem has already presented itself in China (as well as signs that Mao may have been reading Thomas Jefferson!). The Cultural Revolution seemed to be part of the Maoist response to this problem; future Chinese generations no doubt will seek other answers to the problem.

Those in the West who are quick to criticize Mao as a dreamer whose utopian goals for China cannot be realized by Maoist methods have overlooked one factor—change. Mao has said himself that Marx, Engels, and Lenin might look ridiculous a thousand years from now. That can be read as Mao's awareness that the future may bring changes so unexpected and dramatic as to defy classification into such pigeon-holes as "defeats" and "victories."

How does Taiwan fit in the picture of developing trade between the U.S. and the P.R.C.? We believe it was Peking's decision to suspend the urgency of the Taiwan issue which allowed Sino-American rapprochement to go forward as far as it has. This is an important point because it shows how highly Peking values its American connection.

The goal for the moment should be for Washington to improve the substance of its relations with Peking, rather than the form. Full diplomatic relations between Washington and Peking are inevitable and

---

[1] Ross Terrill, *800,000,000: The Real China* (Boston: Little, Brown and Co., 1971).
[2] For a thoughtful treatment of this theme, see Jon Saari's article, "China's Special Modernity," in *China and Ourselves*, ed. Bruce Douglas and Ross Terrill (Boston: Beacon Press, 1971), pp. 65-67.

desirable, but the timing should not be considered urgent. The U.S. is honor-bound not to "dump" Taiwan.

Through all of this discussion of improved ties between the U.S. and the P.R.C., a particular element of perspective is important: the volume of giant mainland China's total foreign trade is only now comparable with that of relatively tiny Taiwan. One fact is, however, highly impressive: Peking's foreign trade has doubled in the last four years.

It is in the realm of the *potential* of P.R.C. trade that the opportunities lie and in which imagination must be applied. It is probable, in our opinion, that by the end of this century, the People's Republic of China will be one of the world's great economic and trading powers.

To take advantage of the changes, challenges, and opportunities that lie within the trade and developmental finance areas of the coming enlarged mutual relationship between Chinese and Americans, we must prepare ourselves much better than we have been doing, both in a bilateral sense and in our awareness of a changing world situation.

There is much to be learned and understood about China, and there is a potential for interaction between the U.S. and China tomorrow that is scarcely imagined anywhere today.

Appendix A
U.S.-CHINA TRADE, 1972-1973

1972

Information for 1972 was obtained from "Trading with the People's Republic of China," *Overseas Business Reports*, U.S. Department of Commerce, May 1973.

U.S. EXPORTS TO CHINA

Commodity	Dollar Value
Wheat (unmilled), including spelt or meslin	32,967,154
Corn or maize (unmilled)	23,022,359
Vegetable oils, fixed & soft (except hydrogenated)	2,199,585
Agricultural machinery, appliances & parts	97,308
Machines for special industries & parts	1,300
Machinery & appliances & machinery parts, nes*	13,996
Electric power machinery, switchgear & parts	216,600
Telecommunications, apparatus & parts	1,679,429
Electrical medical & radiological apparatus	3,000
Road motor vehicles and parts, nes	3,316
Total	$60,205,191

U.S. IMPORTS FROM CHINA

Commodity	Dollar Value
Meat & edible offals, nes, fresh, frozen	31,349
Birds, eggs, albumen, yolks	43,854
Fish (except shellfish), fresh, chilled, frozen	208,118
Fish (except shellfish), salted, dry, smoked	21,904
Shellfish (except prepared or canned)	97,673
Fish in airtight containers & prepared	115,090
Macaroni, noodles, etc.	53,441
Bakery products	4,509
Flour meal, cereal groats, cereal preparations	629
Oranges (except canned mandarin)	303
Citrus fruits, nes	720
Nuts, edible (not for oil)	547,679
Fruits, dried	23,255
Fruits, except glazed, candied, or crystal	1,224

* nes: not elsewhere specified.

Commodity	Dollar Value
Fruits, temporarily preserved	9,126
Fruits & nuts, prepared or preserved, nes	98,561
Vegetables, leguminous, dried	50,234
Vegetables, fresh, chilled, frozen, dried, nes	52,921
Vegetables in temporary preservative	529
Vegetable products, fresh, dried, nes	672
Vegetable & fruit flours, dehydrated, etc.	134,216
Arrowroot, cassava & sago flour & starch	611
Vegetables, prepared or preserved, nes	227,439
Honey	61,055
Sugar confectionery, no cocoa, etc.	22,954
Chocolate, preparations containing cocoa, nes	3,607
Tea, crude or prepared	299,481
Pepper and pimento	121,961
Spices, except pepper and pimento	1,797,169
Food preparations, nes	213,641
Wine, except prune & rice wines	402
Ale, beer, porter, stout	11,155
Beverages, distilled, alcoholic	2,605
Tobacco, unmanufactured	16,520
Chewing & smoking tobacco, snuff	364
Skins (goat & kid), undressed, raw, cured	131,749
Hides & skins, undressed, raw, cured, nes	403
Furskins, undressed	22,462
Groundnuts, including green peanuts	126,519
Soybeans	3,874
Silk waste	24,022
Raw silk	2,422,389
Wool, in grease or washed	25,870
Wool, scored or carbonized	27,286
Fine animal hair, except wool	851,479
Horse & other coarse hair	665,329
Wool, carded or combed, except tops	55,181
Cotton waste	4,213
Clay & other refractory minerals, nes	115,202
Mica, fluorspar, nepheline syenite, etc.	9,002
Minerals, crude, nes	2,000
Bones, ivory, horns, coral & similar products	6,186
Materials of animal origin, nes	7,528,665
Natural gums, resins, balsams, lacs	572
Vegetable materials used for plaiting	2,775
Spices for perfumery, pharmacy, etc., nes	214,327
Nursery stock, bulbs, corns, pips, etc.	1,902
Flowers, buds, foilage, etc. for ornaments	2,726
Other crude vegetable materials, nes	20,816
Mineral waxes	442
Peanut oil	278
Oils, fixed, vegetable, nes	4,497
Organic chemicals	14,540

Inorganic bases, metallic oxides	78,464
Inorganic chemicals except elements, etc.	6,402
Printing ink & benzenoid ink powders	3,837
Prepared paints, enamels, lacquers, etc.	646
Glycosides, glands, organ extracts in bulk	1,441
Medical & pharmaceutical preparations, dosage	12,752
Drugs, nes	70,379
Essential oils and resinoids	302,877
Cosmetics & other toilet preparations, nes	3,438
Soaps	4,884
Pyrotechnical articles	480,791
Plastic materials and shapes, nes	62,877
Albuminoidal substances, starches, etc.	873,504
Wood & resin based chemical products, nes	228,253
Leather, nes	229,793
Furskins, dressed, including dyed	355,734
Rubber tires & tubes for vehicles & aircraft	8,632
Plywood, including wood veneer panels	16,913
Wood manufactures, domestic or decorative use	80,693
Articles manufactured of wood	104,935
Cork manufactures	8,945
Paper & paperboard, nes, in rolls, sheets	572
Paper stationery except correspondence	311
Articles of paper pulp, paper, or paperboard	6,810
Silk yarn and thread	174,184
Cotton fabrics, nes, woven, unbleached	1,496,095
Cotton fabrics, nes, woven, bleached, finished	102,999
Silk fabrics, woven	208,515
Woven fabrics of manmade fibers, nes	13,144
Tulle, lace, ribbons, other small wares	2,399
Coated or impregnated textile fabrics & products	526
Twine, cordage, nets & other manufactures of textile fiber	5,549
Hat bodies	133,492
Wadding, textile fabrics for use in machinery	993
Blankets, including electric & travelling rugs	2,274
Made-up articles of textile materials, nes	388,556
Linoleum and similar floor coverings	721
Carpets and rugs of knotted fabrics	635,779
Carpets, carpeting, and rugs, nes	23,593
Tapestries handwoven or needleworked	39,657
Mats, matting, vegetable plaiting material, etc.	58,912
Building & monument stone, worked & art thereof	31,413
Tile & other nonrefractory ceramic construction materials	4,818
Manufactures of mineral material, nes (except ceramic)	64,657
Articles of ceramic materials, nes	1,611
Glass, drawn or blown, unworked	1,458
Glass containers	3,064
Glass art, nes, including imitation gemstones	112,041
Porcelain or china household wares	534,995
Earthenware, stoneware household art (not ornamental)	104,498
Ceramic & china ornamental articles, nes	20,403

Commodity	Dollar Value
Precious & semiprecious stones (not set), etc., nes	499,557
Aluminum & aluminum alloys, wrought	23,316
Tin & tin alloys, unwrought	638,655
Base metals, unwrought, wrought, waste, scrap, nes	973,720
Containers, metal, for transporting goods	1,873
Hand tools for agriculture or forestry	2,619
Tools, for hand or machine use, nes	22,826
Table flatware and cutlery	17,331
Domestic utensils of base metal	185,611
Household equipment of base metals, nes	255
Articles of base metals, nes	14,224
Domestic appliances & parts, nonelectric	315
Electric power & machinery parts	8,500
Radio receivers & parts, & radio phonographs	4,087
Electric lamps & parts, nes	546
Electrical machinery, apparatus, & parts, nes	20,669
Bicycles and parts	31,593
Pleasure boats, floating structures & parts	941
Lighting fixtures, fittings, & parts	5,775
Furniture	103,084
Travel goods, handbags, personal goods	30,947
Clothing, textile fabric, not knit or crocheted	271,905
Accessories textile fabric, not knit or crocheted	158,644
Clothing and accessories of leather	139,442
Clothing, accessories, etc., knit or crocheted	207,654
Millinery, hats & caps, including materials	19,077
Fur clothing & articles, including artificial	23,546
Footwear, new, except orthopedic	126,480
Cameras, still & flash apparatus, & parts	10,433
Photographic & motion picture equipment, nes	1,863
Medical instruments, etc., except electro-medical	8,074
Measuring, control, etc. instruments, nes	1,815
Motion picture & photo film, exposed, etc.	28,327
Clocks & similar time mechanisms, etc.	21,504
Phonograph records & other sound media	377
Pianos & other string musical instruments, etc.	26,981
Musical instruments, nes	41,564
Parts & accessories for musical instruments	4,545
Maps, charts, books, pamphlets & globes	2,511
Calendars, catalogs, & printed matter, nes	2,683
Rubber and plastic manufactures, nes	22,145
Children's toys, Christmas decorations, etc.	80,260
Fishing & hunting equipment, sports equipment, etc.	19,890
Pens, pencils, nibs, points, crayons, chalk	17,518
Works of art, collector's pieces, antiques	3,487,959
Jewelry, goldsmith's wares, precious metals, etc.	242,687
Jewelry, not precious or semiprecious, costume	46,918
Art & manufactures of carving or molding metal	98,723
Brooms, brushes, dusters, plaiting arts	652,645

Candles, tapers, matches, smoker's art	5,154
Umbrellas & similar articles & parts	9,942
Other manufactured articles, nes	138,174
Special transactions not classed by kind	30,576
Items of estimated value under $251 (formal "etc." entries)	113,300
Total	$32,319,666

1973

Information for 1973 was obtained from the Division of P.R.C. Affairs, Bureau of East-West Trade, U.S. Department of Commerce.

U.S. EXPORTS TO CHINA

Commodity	Dollar Value
Food and live animals	410,084,418
Beverages and tobacco	1,358,611
Crude materials (inedible), except fuel	171,903,018
Mineral fuels, lubricants, etc.	3,475
Oils and fats (animal and vegetable)	19,206,822
Chemicals	7,850,377
Manufactured goods by chief material	9,078,046
Machinery and transport equipment	68,755,884
Miscellaneous manufactured articles, nes	863,126
Total	$689,103,777

U.S. IMPORTS FROM CHINA

Commodity	Dollar Value
Food and live animals	5,973,069
Beverages and tobacco	652,887
Crude materials (inedible), except fuel	14,621,907
Mineral fuels, lubricants, etc.	418,536
Oils and fats (animal and vegetable)	733,719
Chemicals	8,227,165
Manufactured goods by chief material	21,007,798
Machinery and transport equipment	373,150
Miscellaneous manufactured articles, nes	11,157,240
Items not classified by kind	786,442
Total	$63,951,913

Appendix B

A COMPARISON OF SINO-AMERICAN AND SOVIET-AMERICAN TRADE

The figures in this appendix do not include $50.6 million worth of American wheat, corn, and soybeans transshipped through Canada to China during 1973. Thus, the total value of 1973 U.S. exports to China, including the goods shipped through Canada, was $739.7 million, and total two-way trade was $803.4 million. The Canadian transshipments included: 166,205 tons of wheat ($29.8 million), 106,503 tons of corn ($8.8 million), and 49,682 tons of soybeans ($12 million).

SINO-AMERICAN AND SOVIET-AMERICAN TRADE COMPARED
($ millions)

Year	Sino-American	Soviet-American
1971		
U.S. imports	4.9	57.6
U.S. exports	—	161.7
Total	4.9	219.3
1972		
U.S. imports	32.3	95.9
U.S. exports	60.2	550.3
Total	92.5	646.2
1973		
U.S. imports	63.7	215.3
U.S. exports	689.1	1,190.3
Total	752.8	1,405.6
1974—First Quarter		
U.S. imports	20.1	98.9
U.S. exports	343.5	165.3
Total	363.6	264.2
January-April 1974		
U.S. imports	25.6	132.2
U.S. exports	415.6	204.2
Total	441.2	336.4
1974		
U.S. imports	100.0*	420.0*
U.S. exports	1,150.0*	850.0*
Estimated total	1,250.0*	1,270.0*

* Department of Commerce projection.
Source: National Council for U.S.-China Trade, 3 June 1974.

Appendix C
CHINESE FOREIGN TRADE CORPORATIONS

This appendix lists Chinese foreign trade corporations, their addresses, and the commodities and services handled by each. (The information was obtained from U.S. Department of Commerce, "Trading with the People's Republic of China," *Overseas Business Reports*, May 1973.) For assistance in dealing with P.R.C. trade entities contact the Chinese Council for the Promotion of International Trade, Hsi Tan Building, Hsi Chang An Chieh, Peking.

Corporation/Address	Commodities/Services Handled
China National Chemicals Import and Export Co. Erh Li Kou, Hsi Chiao, Peking (Cable: SINO CHEM PEKING)	Rubber, rubber tires, other rubber products, petroleum and petroleum products, chemical fertilizers, insecticides, fungicides, pharmaceuticals, medical apparatus, chemical raw materials, dyestuffs, pigments.
China National Native Produce and Animal By-Products Import and Export Corp. 82 Tung An Men Street, Peking (Cable: CHINA-TUHSU PEKING)	Tea, coffee, cocoa, tobacco, bast fiber, resin, feedingstuffs, timber, forest products, spices, essential oils, patent medicines, medicinal herbs, bristles, horsetails, feathers, down, rabbit hair, wool, cashmere, camel hair, casings, hides, leathers, fur mattresses and other fur products, carpets, down products, living animals.
China National Light Industrial Products Import and Export Corp. 82 Tung An Men Street, Peking (Cable: INDUSTRY PEKING)	Paper, general merchandise, stationery, musical instruments, sporting goods, toys, building materials, electrical appliances, fishnets, net yarns, leather shoes, leather products, pottery and porcelain, human hair, pearls, precious stones and jewelry, ivory and jade carvings, lacquer ware, plaited articles, furniture, artistic handicrafts, handicrafts for daily use.

Corporation/Address	Commodities/Services Handled
China National Textiles Import and Export Corp. 82 Tung An Men Street, Peking (Cable: CHINATEX PEKING)	Cotton, cotton yarns, raw silk, steam filature, wool tops, rayon fibers, synthetic and man-made fibers, cotton piecegoods, woolen piecegoods, linen, wearing apparel, knitted goods, cotton and woolen manufactured goods, ready-made silk articles, drawn works.
China National Cereals, Oils and Foodstuffs Import and Export Corp. 82 Tung An Men Street, Peking (Cable: CEROILFOOD PEKING)	Cereals, edible vegetable and animal oils and fats for industrial use, oil seeds, seeds, oil cakes, feedingstuffs, salt, edible livestock and poultry, meat, and meat products, eggs and egg products, fresh fruits and fruit products, aquatic and marine products, canned goods, sugar and sweets, wines, liquors and spirits, dairy products, vegetables and condiments, bean flour noodles, grain products, canned goods, nuts, dried vegetables.
China National Machinery Import and Export Corp. Erh Li Kou, Hsi Chiao, Peking (Cable: MACHIMPEX PEKING)	Machine tools, presses, diesel engines, gasoline engines, steam turbines, boilers, mining machinery, metallurgical machinery, compressors and pumps, hoists, winches and cranes, transport machinery (motor vehicles) and parts thereof, vessels, agricultural machinery and implements, printing machines, knitting machines, building machinery, machinery for other light industries, ball and roller bearings, tungsten carbide, electric machinery and equipment, telecommunication equipment, electric and electronic measuring instruments, scientific instruments.
China National Metals and Minerals Import and Export Corp. Erh Li Kou, Hsi Chiao, Peking (Cable: MINIMETALS PEKING)	Steel plates, sheets and pipes, steel sections, steel tubes, special steel railway materials, metallic products, pig iron, ferroalloys, nonferrous metals, precious rare metals, ferrous mineral ores, nonferrous mineral ores, nonmetal minerals and products thereof, coal, cement, hardware.

China National Technical Import Corp. Erh Li Kou, Hsi Chiao, Peking (Cable: TECHIMPORT PEKING)	Importation of complete plants and technology.
Sinofracht Chartering and Shipbroking Corp. Erh Li Kou, Hsi Chiao, Peking	Chartering vessels and booking shipping space for Chinese import and export cargoes, similar business on behalf of principals located abroad, canvassing cargoes for shipowners.
Complete Plant Export Corp. Fu-Wai Street, Peking	Export only: complete factories, works and production units (usually, but not exclusively, as part of an economic aid agreement).
Publications Centre Guozi Shudian P.O. Box 399, Peking	Books and periodicals in Chinese and foreign languages, foreign subscriptions to Chinese newspapers and periodicals.
Foreign Trade Transportation Corp. Erh Li Kou, Hsi Chiao, Peking	Customs clearance and delivery of import/export cargoes by land, sea, air and post, clearing and delivering goods in transit through Chinese ports, marine and other insurance (including institution of claims on behalf of cargo owners on request).
People's Insurance Company of China 34 Fan Ti Road, Peking	International trade and marine risk underwriting. (Overseas agents in leading countries.)
China Resources Company Bank of China Building, Des Voeux Road, Central, Hong Kong (Cable: CIRECO HONG KONG)	Represents China National Machinery Import and Export Corp., China National Chemicals Import and Export Corp., China National Metals and Minerals Import and Export Corp., and China National Textile Import and Export Corp.
Ng Fung Hong Bank of China Building, Hong Kong (Cable: NG FUNG HONG KONG)	Represents China National Cereals and Oils and Foodstuffs Import and Export Corp.
Teck Soon Hong Ltd. 37-39 Connaught Road, W. Hong Kong (Cable: STILLION HONG KONG)	Represents China National Native Produce and Animal By-Products Import and Export Corp., China National Light Industrial Products Import and Export Corp., and China National Textiles Import and Export Corp.

Appendix D
U.S. PARTICIPANTS IN THE 1973 FALL CANTON TRADE FAIR

The information in this appendix was obtained from the Bureau of East-West Trade, U.S. Department of Commerce.

Firm or Organization/Address	Representative
W. A. Adams Co., Inc. Oxford, North Carolina	Christian H. Witzke
Alexander Hasenfeld Co. New York, New York	Alexander Hasenfeld (attended on invitation issued to ALKINCO)
Allied Chemical International* 1006 Union House Hong Kong	William Irik Reginald Parsons
Allied Stores Marketing Corp. 401 Fifth Avenue New York, New York	Joachim W. Herbert
B. Altman & Co. New York, New York	n.a.
AMCAL Corporation Box 1414 Charlotte, North Carolina	Ernst J. Beschorner Thomas J. Surrency
Amicale Industries, Inc. 1040 Avenue of the Americas New York, New York	Boris Shlomm
Associate Dry Goods Corp. 415 Fifth Avenue New York, New York	Richard F. Harding J. Arthur Baer II Rudolf E. Kaufman
Associated Merchandise Corp. New York, New York	D. E. Crandall Murray L. Weinberg Martin Newman
Associated Metals & Minerals* 733 Third Avenue New York, New York	Walter J. Simon
J. A. Atwood Corp. 10405 N.E. Thompson Portland, Oregon	James Atwood Mrs. Atwood

* Indicates membership in National Council for U.S.-China Trade.

Firm or Organization/Address	Representative
Baker Trading Co.* P.O. Box 3048 Houston, Texas	J. Ray Pace Martin Klingenberg
Bloomingdale's Lexington at 59th Street New York, New York	Martin Newman Carl Levine Bea Curtis
Caltex Petroleum Corp. 380 Madison Avenue New York, New York	Ray V. D. Gerhart John O. Schneider S. H. Chow
Campus Sweater & Sportswear Co. 3955 Euclid Avenue Cleveland, Ohio	Stanley Polan K. E. Godfrey Stanley Jacobson
Cargill-Tradax Group* Fuji Building No. 2-3, 3 Chome, Marunouchi Chiyoda-ku, Tokyo	Jeremy Liang
Caterpillar Far East, Ltd.* Realty Building, 25th Floor Hong Kong	A. J. Miller (attended on invitation issued to HK Chinese firm, China Engineers)
Cellarmaster, Inc. 604 Sutter Street San Francisco, California	Joe K. Ling
China Bazaar 667 Grant Avenue San Francisco, California	Sinclair Louie
China Consultants International* 3286 M Street, N.W. Washington, D. C.	William Donnett (also represented *American Industrial Report Magazine*)
China Imports (USA) Ltd. 1421 West 132nd Street Gardena, California	S. David Wiessen
China Products, Inc. 410 Nahva Street Honolulu, Hawaii	Koji Ariyoshi
China Products Northwest, Inc. P.O. Box 15245 Seattle, Washington	Ronald Phillips John Mason
China Trade Business Associates* 342 Madison Avenue, Suite 260 New York, New York	Daniel Tretiak Marshall Kaplan
China Trade Corporation* 909 Third Avenue New York, New York	Charles Abrams

Coca-Cola Asia*
810-815 Connaught Center
Hong Kong

Peter W. Fairbarns
Jose F. Suarez

Commercial Metals Co.
3000 Diamond Park Drive
Dallas, Texas

Walter Kammann

Concord Fabrics, Inc.
1411 Broadway
New York, New York

Alvin Weinstein
Mrs. Weinstein

Continental Grain Co.
2 Broadway
New York, New York

Leonard Kuhl

Copen Associates, Inc.
Empire State Building, Suite 5603
New York, New York

Harry Copen
Peter Copen

Cosmos International
488 Madison Avenue
New York, New York

Sidney Brewer (attended on
invitation issued to Dragon
Lady Inc.)

Da Sing Corp.
510 Madison Avenue
New York, New York

Yeh Nan

Desco Shoe Corp.
16 East 34th Street
New York, New York

Robert C. Lipson
(attended on invitation
issued to ALKINCO)

Dow Chemical Pacific, Ltd.
New Henry House, 6th Floor
10 Ice House Street
Hong Kong

Robert Lundeen
Bernard Butcher
James Mackey
Orlo Jantz
James H. Pendergast

Dragon Lady Inc.
1185 Park Avenue
New York, New York

Veronica Yhap

Dresser Industries
Box 560
Olean, New York

John T. Ward
Earl H. Geis
John Murphy
Scott Nickoon

Dynatech (Singapore) Ltd.
27A Jalan Teteram
Singapore 12

Dwight W. Harvie

E. Yuen, Ltd.*
230 Fifth Avenue
New York, New York

E. Belsky
David Muster
Jerry Myerwitz

East Asiatic Co.
New York, New York

Mr. Hansen

Firm or Organization/Address	Representative
Exxon Corporation* 1251 Avenue of the Americas New York, New York	Hubert J. O'Malley M. W. Searls, Jr. (HK) Oliver I. Snapp, Jr. (HK) J. W. Laibe (HK)
Far East Importers, Inc.* P.O. Box 782 Industrial Park Florence, Alabama	Charles C. Anderson Milton Dropo
Fashion Tress, Inc. 750 West 18th Street Hialeah, Florida	Rowland Schaefer
First American Artificial Flower New York, New York	F. Carrady N. Mushinsky David Sharp
First National Bank of Chicago* Chicago, Illinois	A. Robert Abboud (attended on invitation issued to Chicago Chamber of Commerce and Industry)
Floline-Cobid, Ltd. Liu Chong Hing Bank 24 Des Voeux Bank Hong Kong	Alvin Florea
Friendship International 52 Sobin Park Boston, Massachusetts	Lee Sobin
Garfinckel's Washington, D. C.	Lindsay Ely
General Resources, Ltd. 1503 Wing On Central Building 26 Des Voeux Road, Central Hong Kong	John Shoemaker Brian H. Johnson-Hill
Georgia Pacific Corp. 900 S.W. Fifth Avenue Portland, Oregon	William H. Schlauch
Gerli & Co. 155 East 44th Street New York, New York	W. Rhys Cooper
Gimbels New York, New York	David Levitt
Glidden-Durkee (SCM) 900 Union Commerce Building Cleveland, Ohio	G. Keith Brewin Mrs. Brewin

W.R. Grace & Co.   Jack Rimmer
1114 Avenue of the Americas
New York, New York

Gulf & Eastern Trading Corp.   E. Tohari
2039 West First Street, Suite 5   Mrs. Tohari
Fort Myers, Florida

Hercules, Inc.   Robert E. Whitney
Wilmington, Delaware   David Hollingsworth

Home Yardage   Ted Corn
3245 Geary Street   Stan Zimmerman
San Francisco, California

ICD Group, Inc.*   David Cookson
641 Lexington Avenue
New York, New York

IDC Marketing, Inc.   Paul Speltz
2 West 59th Street, Plaza Hotel
New York, New York

ITT   Robert S. M. Chan
Intertrade Development Corp.
1504 Central Building
Hong Kong

Ideal Musical Merchandise Co.   Jack Loeb
149 Fifth Avenue   Mrs. Loeb
New York, New York

International Corp. of America*   C. J. Wang
P.O. Box 363
Washington, D. C.

Byron Jackson, Inc.   R. F. Meiklejohn
6505 Paramount Boulevard   Paul Brown
Long Beach, California   (attended on invitation
                                          issued to Baker Trading Co.)

Kaiser Trading Co.*   Cornell C. Maier
300 Lakeside Drive   E. Allen Holbrook
Oakland, California   Marvin L. Lee

Alfred Klugmann International   Julius Klugmann
43 West 16th Street, Suite 300
New York, New York

Knitastiks   Martin Marlowe
610 Star House
Kowloon, Hong Kong

Koch International Trading Co.   Herbert G. Roskind, Jr.
892 Wayne Industrial Park, Route 9
Wellesley Hills, Massachusetts

Firm or Organization/Address	Representative
Kraftco Corp. Kraftco Court Glenview, Illinois	William O. Beers (attended on invitation issued to Chicago Chamber of Commerce & Industry)
Albert Lee Co. 2520 South Curson Avenue Los Angeles, California	Albert Lee
Levi Strauss (Far East) Room 70, Tung Ying Building 100 Nathan Road Kowloon, Hong Kong	Jack Street Mary Street Oliver Wood (attended on invitation issued to Levi Strauss (FE) Macau Ltd.)
C. W. Loyd Co., Inc. P10 Box 190 South Pittsburgh, Tennessee	C. W. Loyd
Charles Lubin Company 31 West 21st Street New York, New York	Milton J. Bordin Dorothy Lubin
Lubman & Co. 2915 Avalon Court Berkeley, California	Stanley Lubman Mrs. Lubman (attended on invitation issued to California Chamber of Commerce)
Magid Glove Mfg. Co., Inc. 2201 Wabansia Avenue Chicago, Illinois	David Cohen Mrs. Cohen
Manca Import-Export Co. 222 Westlake Avenue North Seattle, Washington	Charles B. Manca
Marshall Field & Co. 111 North State Street Chicago, Illinois	John Richert Robert Hoffman
May Company 801 South Broadway Los Angeles, California	Richard L. Boje Elaine Pasternack Carol Marchetti (N.Y. office)
May Lee Industries* 475 Park Avenue South New York, New York	Richard Louie Richard J. Wood Thomas O. Caylor
N. A. Maya Import-Export P.O. Box 4999 Miami Beach, Florida	N. A. Maya
Men's Wear International 350 Fifth Avenue, Suite 4810 New York, New York	Ed Fahrenkopf

Mill Valley Trading Co. 12 Shell Road Mill Valley, California	Herb Newman
Mobil Oil Hong Kong, Ltd.* Prince's Building, 18/F Hong Kong	Everett Checket John J. Soong
Monsanto Far East, Ltd.* Management House 26 Canal Road West Hong Kong	Keith A. Hoy George Chew John H. Tung
Montgomery Ward 619 West Chicago Avenue Chicago, Illinois	S. N. Doolittle
NAICTO 1450 Broadway New York, New York	Edwin Sedran Mrs. Sedran
North Carolina Tobacco Assn. The York Building Raleigh, North Carolina	Ed Skinner
Overseas Marketing Enterprises P.O. Box 169 Stockton, California	Meyer Lewis Mrs. Lewis
Peking Art Rug Co. 79/81 Austin Road Kowloon, Hong Kong	Mrs. Rita T. Lou
Peking Commodities 1115 Broadway New York, New York	Brian M. Anderson
Peking Imports & Manufactures 1115 Broadway New York, New York	Thomas C. Farugia
J. C. Penney Co., Inc. 1301 Avenue of the Americas New York, New York	Robert Gill Robert Boulogne
Pfizer Asia 1 Stubbs Road Hong Kong	Lawrence T. Higgs
Phillips Petroleum Co. 80 Broadway New York, New York	Claudio Galvis Joe J. Tanner
Pirouette Imports, Inc. 47 West 34th Street New York, New York	Manny Hamowy Mrs. Hamowy
Henry Pollak, Inc. 1410 Broadway New York, New York	Henry Pollak Mrs. Pollak

Firm or Organization/Address	Representative
Pyrotechnics Corporation 2349 West La Palma Anaheim, California	W. Patrick Moriarity
H. Reisman Corp. 377 Crane Street Orange, New Jersey	William J. McFarland
R. J. Reynolds Tobacco Co. Winston-Salem, North Carolina	W. Stuart Leake
Rollway Bearing Co. Syracuse, New York	Louis R. Muller
S&S Machinery Co. 140 53rd Street Brooklyn, New York	Simon Srybnik Judith Markowitz
Saks Fifth Avenue New York, New York	Roger Goring
E. L. Scott & Co., Inc. One World Trade Center, 2347 New York, New York	E. L. Scott, Jr.
Sears, Roebuck & Co. Sears Tower Chicago, Illinois	Ira Quint K. C. Kunze E. Kaufman
Skyline Manufacturing Co., Inc. 19 West 34th Street New York, New York	Al Goldberg
Singer* 30 Rockefeller Plaza New York, New York	Alexander Dunbar Mahlon R. Saibel (HK office)
Smith International 4467 MacArthur Boulevard Newport Beach, California	A. M. Birnie
Sobin Chemicals, Inc. Sobin Park Boston, Massachusetts	Julian Sobin Keith S. Wood
Spinnerin Yarn Co., Inc. 230 Fifth Avenue New York, New York	Donald Blick
Spring Mills, Inc. 1430 Broadway New York, New York	M. C. Lanford
Steelmet, Inc. 1204 Grant Building Pittsburgh, Pennsylvania	Alan Amper

Swirles & Co. 900 North Alvarado Los Angeles, California	Frank M. Swirles
Tar Residuals, Inc. 565 Fifth Avenue New York, New York	Charles H. Makovec
Teters Floral Co. Bolivar, Missouri	H. Tiffin Teters
Tidewater Marine Services, Inc. 3308 Tulane Avenue New Orleans, Louisiana	Sam S. Allgood
Trade World 70 Bridge Street Newton, Massachusetts	Francis J. Callahan
U.S.-China Trade Corp.* 2 Penn Plaza New York, New York	Wallace Chavkin Robert Bloom
U.S. Steel International* 100 Church Street New York, New York	Aubrey W. Fitch, Jr. T. M. Harvey
George Uhe Co., Inc. 76 Ninth Avenue New York, New York	George Uhe C. Lloyd Fishback
Union Carbide Asia Ltd.* Prince's Building Charter Road, Hong Kong	Kenneth E. Lamb Robert M. Lambert Bob Wheatley
Uniroyal Chemical 1230 Avenue of the Americas New York, New York	James F. O'Hearn
Universal Leaf Tobacco, Inc. Richmond, Virginia	Stuart G. Christian, Jr. Norton Howe, Jr.
Valley Nitrogen Producers, Inc. 1221 Van Ness Avenue Fresno, California	Warren H. Brock (invitation issued to California Chamber of Commerce)
Westinghouse Electric Corp.* Gateway Center Pittsburgh, Pennsylvania	F. Anthony Mrs. Anthony J. G. Deley Keith Johnson
Weyerhauser Co. Tacoma, Washington	Gerritt Wielenga Robert Rice (HK office) Richard Lucas (HK office)
Wooster Brush Co. Wooster, Ohio	Henry C. Lee Mrs. Lee

Firm or Organization/Address	Representative
Paul Yang Associates 251 South Lake Avenue, Suite 811 Pasadena, California	Paul Yang
Zeitlin & Co. Philadelphia, Pennsylvania	Arthur R. Spector Mrs. Spector
Charles Zucker Corp. 31-33 Mercer Street New York, New York	Bob Borella
Oliver (U.S.) Boston, Massachusetts	Dana I. Robinson
U.S.-China Chamber of Commerce 1700 Pennsylvania Avenue, N.W. Washington, D. C.	Robert Fillet
California Chamber of Commerce 455 Capitol Hill Sacramento, California	Warren Brock Stanley Lubman
Chicago Chamber of Commerce and Industry Chicago, Illinois	A. Robert Abboud William O. Beers
China American Relations Society Suite 1400 25 West 43rd Street New York, New York	Thomas Manton
Harned Pettus Hoose 129 N. Rockingham Avenue Los Angeles, California	
Hua Chiao Commercial Bank 92 Queen's Road Central Hong Kong	Mr. and Mrs. C. K. Chan
International Intertrade Index 744 Broad Street Newark, New York	John E. Felber
ABC News New York	Desmond Wong
The New York Times Sutherland House Hong Kong	Ian Stewart
Newsweek 2 Kennedy Terrace Hong Kong	Loren Jenkins
Journal of Commerce Hong Kong	Paul Strauss

Time-Life
205 Prince's Building
Hong Kong

David Aikman

U.S. Liaison Office
Peking

Herbert E. Horowitz
William F. Rope

U.S. Consulate General
Hong Kong

Linwood R. Starbird
Robert M. Perito

P.R.C. Division
Bureau of East-West Trade
Department of Commerce
Washington, D. C.

William Clarke

Voice of America
Hong Hong

John Schultz

National Council for U.S.-China Trade

Mr. and Mrs. Eugene Theroux
Arnie de Keyser
Mr. and Mrs. D. C. Burnham,
Westinghouse Electric Corp.
Mr. and Mrs. Christopher H.
Phillips, President, NCUSCT
Mr. and Mrs. William A. Hewitt,
Deere & Co.
Mr. and Mrs. Gabriel Hauge,
Manufacturers Hanover Trust
Mr. and Mrs. Walter S. Surrey,
Surrey, Karaski & Morse
Mr. and Mrs. Andrew E. Gibson,
Interstate Oil Transport Co.
Mr. and Mrs. Fred M. Seed,
Cargill, Inc.
Mr. and Mrs. William M. Batten,
J. C. Penney Co.
Mr. and Mrs. Charles H. Weaver,
Westinghouse Electric Corp.

Bibliography

Books and Articles

Barnett, A. Doak. *China After Mao*. Princeton: Princeton University Press, 1967.

————. *Uncertain Passage*. Washington, D.C.: The Brookings Institution, 1974.

Barnett, A. Doak, and Reischauer, Edwin O. *The United States and China: The Next Decade*. New York: Praeger, 1970.

Boarman, Patrick M., ed. *Trade With China*. Los Angeles: Center for International Business, 1973.

Cahill, Henry A. *The China Trade and U.S. Tariffs*. New York: Praeger, 1973.

Chao, Kang. *The Construction Industry in Communist China*. Chicago: Aldine, 1968.

Chen, Nai-Ruenn, and Galenson, Walter. *The Chinese Economy Under Communism*. Chicago: Aldine, 1969.

Cheng, Chu-Yuan. *The Machine Building Industry in Communist China*. Chicago: Aldine, 1971.

Clavell, James. *Tai-Pan*. New York: Atheneum, 1966.

Clubb, O. Edmund. *China and Russia: The Great Game*. New York: Columbia University Press, 1971.

Cohen, Jerome A. *Chinese Law and Sino-American Trade*. Harvard Law School Studies in Chinese Law No. 15. Cambridge: Harvard University Press, 1971.

Crossman, Carl L. *The China Trade*. Princeton: Pyne Press, 1972.

Davies, John Paton, Jr. *Dragon by the Tail*. New York: W. W. Norton, 1972.

Dawson, Owen L. *Communist China's Agriculture*. New York: Praeger, 1970.

Domes, Jurgen. *The Internal Politics of China, 1949-1972*. New York: Praeger, 1973.

Eckstein, Alexander, ed. *China Trade Prospects and U.S. Policy.* New York: Praeger, 1971.

Fairbank, John King. *Trade and Diplomacy on the China Coast: The Opening of the Treaty Ports, 1842-1854.* Rev. ed. Stanford: Stanford University Press, 1969.

Hao, Yen-ping. *The Comprador in Nineteenth Century China.* Cambridge: Harvard University Press, 1970.

Hersh, Marc, and Lent, Michael. *Trade With China.* New York: Pan American World Airways, 1971.

Hsiao, Gene T. "Communist China's Foreign Trade Contracts and Means of Settling Disputes." *Vanderbilt Law Review,* vol. 20 (March 1967).

————. "Communist China's Trade Treaties and Agreements (1949-1964)." *Vanderbilt Law Review,* vol. 21 (October 1968).

Hsu, Immanuel C. Y. *The Rise of Modern China.* New York: Oxford University Press, 1970.

Japan External Trade Organization (JETRO). *How to Approach the China Market.* Tokyo: Press International, 1972.

Kahn, Herman, and Weiner, Anthony. *The Year 2000.* New York: Macmillan, 1967.

Karnow, Stanley. *Mao and China: From Revolution to Revolution.* New York: Viking, 1972.

Lall, Arthur S. *How Communist China Negotiates.* New York: Columbia University Press, 1968.

Lee, Luke T. *China and International Agreements.* Durham, N. C.: Rules of Law Press, 1969.

Li, Victor H. "Legal Aspects of Trade with Communist China." *Columbia Journal of Transnational Law,* vol. 3 (1964).

Lindbeck, John M. H., ed. *China: Management of a Revolutionary Society.* Seattle: University of Washington Press, 1971.

Liu, Jung-Chao. *China's Fertilizer Economy.* Chicago: Aldine, 1970.

Mah, Feng-Hwa. *Foreign Trade of Mainland China.* Chicago: Aldine, 1971.

Mehnart, Klaus. *China Returns.* New York: E. P. Dutton, 1971.

Metcalf, John E. *China Trade Guide.* New York: First National City Bank, 1972.

Nagel's Encyclopedia-Guide: China. Geneva, 1969.

Richman, Barry. *Industrial Society in Communist China.* New York: Random House, 1969.

Sheeks, Robert B., and Wu, Yuan-li. *The Organization and Support of Scientific Research and Development in Mainland China.* New York: Praeger, 1970.

Snow, Edgar. *Red China: The Other Side of the River.* Rev. ed. New York: Random House, 1970.

Stahnke, Arthur A. *China's Trade with the West: A Political and Economic Analysis.* New York: Praeger, 1972.

Stark, Steven R. "An Analysis of the Foreign Trade Practices of the People's Republic of China Including Comments on the Canadian Experience." *University of British Columbia Law Review,* vol. 5 (1970).

Terrill, Ross. *800,000,000: The Real China.* Boston: Little, Brown, 1971.

U.S. Central Intelligence Agency. *People's Republic of China: Atlas.* Washington, D.C.: Government Printing Office, 1971.

U.S. Congress, Joint Economic Committee. *Economic Profile of Mainland China.* New York: Praeger, 1968.

U.S. Congress, Joint Economic Committee. *People's Republic of China: An Economic Assessment.* Washington, D. C.: Government Printing Office, 1972.

U.S. Congress, Senate, Committee on Foreign Relations. *China and the United States, Today and Yesterday: Hearings.* Washington, D. C.: Government Printing Office, 1972.

————. *United States Relations with the People's Republic of China: Hearings.* Washington, D. C.: Government Printing Office, 1971.

U.S. Department of Commerce. "Trading with the People's Republic of China." *Overseas Business Reports,* OBR 73-16, 1973.

Whitson, William W. *The Chinese High Command: A History of Communist Military Politics, 1927-72.* New York: Praeger, 1973.

————. *Doing Business With China: American Trade Opportunities in the 1970s.* New York: Praeger, 1974.

Willmott, W. E., ed. *Economic Organization in Chinese Society.* Stanford: Stanford University Press, 1972.

Wu, Yuan-li, ed. *China: A Handbook.* New York: Praeger, 1973.

Periodicals

The China Letter. Published monthly by The Asia Letter Ltd., P.O. Box 3477 Sheungwan, Hong Kong, or P.O. Box 54149, Los Angeles, California 90054.

The China Quarterly. Published by the Contemporary China Institute, 24 Fitzray Square, London, W.I.

China Trade Report. Published monthly by the Far Eastern Economic Review, Ltd., P.O. Box 160, Hong Kong.

Current Scene. Chun Shun Building, 13115 Gordon Rd., Hong Kong.

The Far Eastern Economic Review. Published weekly by Far Eastern Economic Review, Ltd., P.O. Box 160, Hong Kong.

U.S.-China Business Review. Published every other month by the National Council for U.S.-China Trade, Suite 513, 1100 17th St., N.W., Washington, D. C. 20036.